This Text Book is useful for Sir Parashurambhau College of Arts, Science and Commerce, Pune. (Autonomous)

Sociology
Introduction to Sociology : Perspectives and Themes

F.Y. B. A. (Sem. - II) (Course Code : SO1246)

Prin. Dr. Vijay M. Jadhav
(M.A., B.Ed., M.Phil., Ph.D.)
Shri Banshwar Shikshan Sansthas Arts, Science & Commerce College, Burhanagar, Ahmednagar.

Dr. Gulab Pathan
(M.A., B.Ed., M.Phil., Ph.D.)
Head Department of Sociology, Poona College of Arts, Science and commerce, Pune. Camp.

2023

Price: 100/-

SUCCESS PUBLICATIONS

Published by
Dr. Rajesh M. Patne
Success Publications
Radha Krishna Apartment, 535, Shaniwar Peth,
Appa Balwant Chowk, Opp. Prabhat Talkies, Pune - 411 030.
Ph. 24434662. Mobile: 9325315464.

Printed at
Success Publications
S.No. 30/27, Laxmi Industrial Estate,
Near Prabhat News Paper, Dhayari, Pune-41.

Edition
2023

Edited By
Mr. Valmik Gaikwad

Typesetting, Layout
Mr. Valmik Gaikwad

Cover Designing
Miss. Varsha Lokhande

ISBN NO. – 978-93-93220-95-0

Preface

It is a matter of great pleasure for us to present this book to our esteemed readers. This book has been designed as standard text on 'Introduction to Sociology : Perspectives and Themes' for F.Y.B.A. (Sem. - II).

This book comprehensively covers the entire syllabus of F.Y.B.A. (Sem. - II) Course of Sir Parashurambhau College (Autonomous), Pune effective from 2019 onwards. It has been written to meet the requirements of students of F.Y.B.A. (Sem. - II) Some of the special features of the book are as follows:

1. *Full coverage of the revised syllabus of F.Y.B.A. (Sem. - II).*
2. *Chapter outline at the beginning of each chapter to give a bird's eye view of the topics covered in the chapter.*
3. *Point wise explanation of each topic in the chapter.*
4. *Topics are logically arranged in numbered paragraphs exactly according to the modified syllabus.*
5. *Proposed questions at the end of each chapter.*
6. *Extensive use of diagrams, tables and various forms to give visual view of key concepts and techniques.*
7. *Conversational, lucid and simple language.*

Every effort has been made to provide the readers with most up-to-date and authentic material on the subject.

We are very grateful to our publisher Mrs. and Mr. Rajesh Patne who have rendered all possible assistance in bringing out this book. We wish to acknowledge our deep gratitude to staff who have assisted and helped us in preparing this book. We will consider our efforts amply rewarded in case the book proves useful to the students and teachers of the subject.

Suggestions of readers are welcome and shall be acknowledged with gratitude.

With best wishes.

By Authors

Syllabus

F.Y.B.A. (Sem. - II) (Course Code : SO1246)

Sociology (Introduction to Sociology : Perspectives and Themes)

Unit No.	Topic	Lectures
1	**Introduction to Sociology Perspectives:** a) Structural-function: Talcott Parson's 'AGIL model' b) Conflict: Karl Marx's theory of 'Class Struggle' c) Feminist: Gilman theory of 'Gender Inequality'	12
2	**Social Stratification and Mobility:** a) Social Stratification: Meanings, characteristics b) Forms of Stratification: Caste, Class, Gender, Power c) Social Mobility: Meaning and Forms. d) Perspectives on Social Stratification	12
3	**Communication and Mass Media:** a) Social Change: Meaning and Factors b) Mass Media: Meaning and types (Print, Electronic and Social Media) c) Impact of Mass Media on Society	12
4	**Application of Sociology:** b) Applied Sociology: Meaning, and Scope of Applied Sociology. c) Career with Sociology: NGO, Social Work, Social Welfare, Labour Welfare, Corporate Sector, Civil Services, Law, Correctional administration, Distance Management, Journalism, Human Resources Management.	12

INDEX

F.Y.B.A. (Sem. - II) (Course Code : SO1246)
Sociology (Introduction to Sociology : Perspectives and Themes)

UNIT 1

Introduction to Sociology Perspectives

Introduction:

The basic insight of sociology is that human behavior is shaped by the groups to which people belong and by the social interaction that take place within those groups. We are who we are and we behave the way we do because we happen to live in a particular society at a particular point in space and time. People tend to accept their social world unquestioningly, as something "natural." But the sociological perspective enables us to see society as a temporary social product, created by human beings and capable of being changed by them as well. The sociological perspective invites us to look at our familiar surroundings in a fresh way. It encourages us to take a new look at the world we have always taken for granted, to examine our social environment with the same curiosity that we might bring to an exotic foreign culture. The study of sociology leads us into areas of society that we might otherwise have ignored or misunderstood. Since our world view is shaped by our personal experience and since people with different social experiences have different definitions of social reality, sociology helps us to appreciate viewpoints other than our own and to understand how these viewpoints came into being.

1.1 Structural-Functional Perspective:

The structural-functional approach is a perspective in sociology that sees society as a complex system whose parts work together to promote solidarity and stability. It asserts that our lives are guided by social structures, which are relatively stable patterns of social behavior. Social structures give shape to our lives - for example, in families, the community, and through religious organizations. And certain rituals, such as a handshake or complex religious ceremonies, give structure to our everyday lives. Each social structure has social functions, or consequences for the operation of society as a whole. Education, for example, has several important functions in a society, such as socialization, and learning. Functionalism also states that society is like an organism, made up of different parts that work together. Thus one of the key ideas in Structural Functionalism is that society is made-up of groups or institutions, which are cohesive, share common norms, and have a definitive culture. Robert K. Merton argued that functionalism is about the more static or concrete aspects of society, institutions like government or religions. However, any group large enough to be a social institution is included in Structural Functionalist thinking, from religious values to sports clubs and everything in between. Structural Functionalism explains that the way society is organized is the most natural and efficient way for it to be organized.

1.1.1 Talcott Parson's AGIL Model:

The AGIL paradigm is a sociological scheme created by American sociologist Talcott Parsons in the 1950s. It is a systematic depiction of certain societal functions, which every society must meet to be able to maintain stable social life. The AGIL paradigm is part of Parsons's larger action theory, outlined in his notable book *The Structure of Social Action*, in *The Social System* and in later works, which aims to construct a unified map of all action systems, and ultimately "living systems". Indeed, the actual AGIL system only appeared in its first elaborate form in 1956, and Parsons extended the system in various layers of complexity during the rest of his intellectual life. Towards the end of his life, he added a new dimension to the action system, which he called the paradigm of the human condition; within that paradigm, the action system occupied the integral dimension.

A) The Functional Prerequisites of Action Systems (Including the Social System):

Parsons' theory is a part of the paradigm of action theory. AGIL represents the functional scheme for the whole general action system (including the human condition paradigm), so that AGIL also defines the cultural system, the personality system etc. The social system represents the integral part of the action system and is in this way only a subsystem within the greater whole of systems. For example the order of the cultural system vis-à-vis the AGIL functional scheme is:

A: Cognitive symbolization. G: Expressive symbolization. I: Moral-evaluative symbolization. L: Constitutive symbolization.

Society, in this paradigm, is defined as prototypical category of the social system that meets the essential functional prerequisites that define the system's universal attributes. AGIL scheme outlines four systematic, core functions that are prerequisites for any society to be able to persist over time. It is a misconception that the system functions are "institutions," they exist on a much higher level of theoretical comprehension than institutions yet each system is inhabited by institutions. Institutions have either universal implications or historical implications depending on their form, nature and specification. The system shapes the "nature" of its institutions so that the political system is the orbit of "political institutions." The stock-market is common-sensically not regarded as a political institution yet the stock-market might have political functions (which is a different analytical issue).

AGIL is an acronym from the initials of each of the four systemic necessities. The AGIL system is considered a cybernetic hierarchy and has generally the following order L-I-G-A, when the order is viewed from an "informational" point of view; this implies that the L function could "control" or define the I function (and the I the G and so on) approximately in the way in which a computer-game-program "defines" the game. The program does not "determine" the game (which actual outcome would depend on the input of the player that was what Parsons in a sense called the voluntaristic aspect of action) but it "determined" the logical parameter of the game, which lies implicit in the game's concrete design and rules. In this way, Parsons would say that culture would not determine the social system but it would "define it." The AGIL system had also an energy side (or a "conditional" side), which would go A-G-I-L. So that the Adaptive level would be on the highest level of the cybernetic hierarchy from the energy or "conditional" point of view. However, within these two reverse sequences of the hierarchy Parsons maintained that in the long historical perspective, a system which was high in information (that is, a system that followed the L-I-G-A sequence) would tend to prevail over system which was high in energy. For example in the human body, the DNA is the informational code which will tend to control "the body" which is high in energy. Within the action system, Parsons would maintain that it was culture which was highest in information and which in his way was in cybernetic control over other components of the action system, as well as the social system. However, it is important to maintain that all action systems (including social systems) are always depending on the (historically specific) equilibrium of the overall forces of information and condition, which both shape the outcome of the system. Also it is important to highlight that the AGIL system does not "guarantee" any historical system survival; they rather specify the minimum conditions for whether societies or action systems in principle can survive. Whether a concrete action system survives or not is a sheer historical question.

1) **Adaptation**, or the capacity of society to interact with the environment. This includes, among other things, gathering resources and producing commodities to social redistribution.

2) **Goal Attainment**, or the capability to set goals for the future and make decisions accordingly. Political resolutions and societal objectives are part of this necessity.

3) **Integration**, or the harmonization of the entire society is a demand that the values and norms of society are solid and sufficiently convergent. This requires, for example, the religious system to be fairly consistent, and even in a more basic level, a common language.

4) **Latency**, or latent pattern maintenance, challenges society to maintain the integrative elements of the integration requirement above. This means institutions like family and school, which mediate belief systems and values between an older generation and its successor.

These four functions aim to be intuitive. For example a tribal system of hunter-gatherers needs to gather food from the external world by hunting animals and gathering other goods. They need to have a set of goals and a system to make decisions about such things as when to migrate to better hunting grounds. The tribe also needs to have a common belief system that enforces actions and decisions as the community sees fit. Finally there needs to be some kind of educational system to pass on hunting and gathering skills and the common belief system. If these prerequisites are met, the tribe can sustain its existence.

B) Systematic Depiction of AGIL Functions:

The four functions of AGIL break into external and internal problems, and further into instrumental and consummatory problems. External problems include the use of natural resources and making decisions to achieve goals, whereas keeping the community integrated and maintaining the common values and practices over succeeding generations are considered internal problems. Furthermore, goal attainment and the integral function belong to the consummatory aspect of the systems. It is common to use a table to illustrate the four functions and their differences in spatial and temporal orientation. (The following only addresses the AGIL component examples for the social system for example; "political office" is not a unit for the categories on the action-system level).

	Instrumental functions	**Consummatory functions**
External problems	*Adaptation* - natural resources - commodity production	*Goal-attainment* - political offices - common goals
Internal problems	*Latency (or Pattern Maintenance)* - family - schools	*Integration* - religious systems - media

Each of the four individual functional necessities is further divided into four sub-categories. The four sub-categories are the same four functions as the major four AGIL categories and so on. Hence one subsystem of the societal community is the category of "citizenship," which is a category we today would associate with the concept of civil society. In this way, citizenship (or civil society) represents according to Parsons, the goal-attainment function within the subsystem of the Societal Community. For example, a community's adaption to the economic environment might consist of the basic "industrial" process of production (adaption), political-strategic goals for production (goal-attainment), the interaction between the economical system and the societal community, which integrates production mechanisms both in regard to economic as well as societal factors (integration), and common cultural values in their "selective" relevance for the societal-economic interchange process (latency (or Pattern Maintenance)). Each of these systemic processes will (within the scope of the cybernetic hierarchy) is regulated by what Talcott Parsons calls generalized symbolic media. Each system level of the general action-paradigm has each their set of generalized symbolic media (so that the set of generalized symbolic media for the social system is not identical with those of the action system or those of the human condition paradigm). In regard to the social system, there are the following four generalized symbolic media:

A: (Economy): Money. G: (Political system): Political power. I: (Societal Community): Influence. L: (Judiciary system): Value-commitment.

C) Criticism of the AGIL Scheme:

Parsons' theory has been criticised as being too abstract to be used constructively in any significant empirical research. While the four functions of the AGIL scheme are intuitive and many social systems can be described according to the paradigm of Parsons' structural functionalism, one can question the utility that such an inspection brings to a scientific sociological study. Defenders of the AGIL scheme respond that there have indeed been situations where social systems, such as some industries, have failed to operate because they have neglected one or more of the four functions. Hence, the AGIL scheme can be tested against political or economical systems in operation to see if they meet the criteria. Defenders also highlight that all theoretical systems are abstract (indeed modern physics uses extremely high levels of theoretical abstractions (without anyone "protesting")). Any good theoretical system has to be abstract, since this is the meaning and function of theoretical systems. Another notable criticism attacks the AGIL schemes' failure to take historical change into account. Critics argue that Parsons' theory is inexcusably static and lacks the flexibility to meet instances of social change. While Parsons purports that the AGIL scheme is a general theory of social functions that can be applied to any social system at any time or place in the history of humankind, critics contend that it is basically just a model of the post-war United States, or, moreover, merely an ideal social structure of the middle-class of United States. Parsons' defenders argue that such criticisms are misplaced inasmuch as Parsons tried to identify the most important systemic features of any society whatsoever: *any* society would need to meet the functions indicated by AGIL, even if it used different institutions or arrangements for doing so. Moreover, Parsons himself tried to develop a theory of world history, and to explain social change through his system, although his critics have suggested that this amounts to little more than window-dressing. Nevertheless, despite recent sympathetic reappraisals, Parsons no longer dominates Anglophone social theory in the way he once did.

1.2 Conflict Perspective:

In the 19th century, a German philosopher named Karl Marx began exploring the relationship between economy and the workers within that system. Over his lifetime, Marx developed a theory that human societies progress though a struggle between two distinct social classes. The proletariat, the workers, is the lower class. They perform the labor, but the upper class managers, bosses, and rulers, called the bourgeoisie, get the profits. In this system, which became known as Marxism, governments existed to protect the wealthy, not the common good.

To arrive at this conclusion, Marx studied and wrote on philosophy, economy, and politics. Marx formulated these into a scientific study of society. Thus, he is considered to be one of the founding figures of sociology as a discipline. Marx believed that with a mixture of historical research and scientific methods, society could be analyzed logically and rationally. This idea, of course, is still followed by sociologists today.

1.2.1 Karl Marx's Theory of Class Struggle:

Marx's sociology is in fact, sociology of class struggle. According to Bendex and Lipset, "A social class in Marx's terms is any aggregate of persons who perform the same function in the organization of production." According to Marx, "Class is the manifestation of economic differentiation."

A) Concept of Class Struggle:

The concept of class struggle, though not originally propounded by Karl Marx, is yet one of his great contributions to Sociology. To Marx, "the history of all hitherto existing society is the history of class struggle." (The first line of communist manifesto (1848) reads.) According to Raymond Aron, "the classes are the principal actors in the historical drama of capitalism in particular and of history in general."

Classes refer to the groups of people having their own role to play in the relations of production. Relations of production refer to the fact that in the process of industrial production the labour and capital stands in specific relation to each other. Labour is the capacity which the working class possesses. Capital is the instrument invested out of which profit is derived. Those who possess capital they are the owners of capital. Those who are labourers they are the owners of labour power. Capital gets profit, labour gets wage. Labour and capital are interrelated, they are inseparable. One cannot be thought of without the other. Marx says:

"Classes are hence the groups of people identified and distinguished from each other on the basis of their relations to the economic means of production. Economic means of production refers to the economic infrastructure that few people own as against many. Few people are capitalists and many are labourers. Economic infrastructure refers to all those land, machinery, tools, technology and the skills that assist the process of production."

B) The Class Structure:

The word "class" originated from the Latin term "Classis" a group called to arms, a division of the people. In the rule of legendary Roman king, Servius Tullius (678-534 B.C), the Roman society was divided into five classes or orders according to their wealth. Subsequently the word 'class' was applied to large groups of people into which human society came to be divided.

Marx recognized class as a unique feature of capitalist societies. Marx has used the term Social class throughout his works but explained it only in a fragmented form. The clearest passages on the concept of class structure can be found in the third volume of his famous work Capital (1894). Under the title of "Social classes", Marx distinguished three classes related to the three sources of income.

1) Owners of simple labour power or labourers whose main source of income is labour.
2) Owners of capital or capitalists whose main source of income is profit or surplus value.
3) Landowners whose main source of income is ground rent.

In this way the class structure of modern capitalist society is composed of three major classes" i.e. salaried labourers of workers, capitalists and landowners. At a broader level, society could be divided into two major classes—Haves and Have-nots. Haves are the owners of land/or capital often called as Bourgeoisie and the Have-nots are those who own nothing but their own labour power, often called as Proletariates. According to Marx, "a social class occupies a fixed place in the process of production." Bendex and Lipset have identified five variables that determine a class in the Marxian sense:

a) Conflicts over the distribution of economic rewards between the classes.
b) Easy communication between the individuals in the same class position so that ideas and action programs are readily disseminated.
c) Growth of class consciousness in the sense that the members of the class have a feeling of solidarity and understanding of their historical role.
d) Profound dissatisfaction in the lower class over its inability to control the economic structure of which it feels itself to be the exploited victim.
e) Establishment of a political organization resulting from the economic structure, the historical situation and maturation of class-consciousness.

C) Criteria for Determination of Class:

A social class has two major criteria:

1) Objective Criteria:

People sharing the same relationship to the means of production comprise a class. For example, all labourers have a similar relationship with the land owners. On the other hand all the landowners as a class have a similar relationship with the land and labourers. In this way, labourers on one hand and land owners on the other hand could be seen as classes.

However, for Marx, this relationship is not sufficient to determine the class. Because according to him it is not sufficient for class to be "Class in itself" but it should also be "Class for itself". Marx means by "Class in itself" the objective criteria of any social class. He is not satisfied with the objective criteria. Hence, he equally emphasizes upon the other major criteria i.e. "Class for itself" or the subjective criteria.

2) Subjective Criteria:

Any collectivity of human grouping with a similar relationship would make a category not a class, if subjective criteria are not included. The members of any one class not only have similar consciousness but they also share a similar consciousness of the fact that they belong to the same class.

This similar consciousness of a class serves as the basis for uniting its members for organising social action. Here this similar consciousness towards acting together for their common interest is what Marx class-"Class for itself." In this way these two criteria together determine a class and class structure in any given society.

D) Classification of Societies in History and Emergence of Classes:

Marx differentiated stages of human history on the basis of their economic regime or modes of production. He distinguished four major modes of production:

i) The Asiatic

ii) The Ancient

iii) The Feudal

iv) The Capitalistic

He predicted that all social development will culminate into a stage called Communism. He simplified this classification of societies or various stages of human history into:

1) The Primitive:

Communal system was the first and the lowest form of organization of people. It existed for thousands of years. Man started using primitive tools like sticks and stones for hunting and food gathering. Gradually man improved these tools. He learned to make fire, cultivation and animal husbandry. In this system of very low level of forces of production, the relations of production were based on common ownership of the means of production. Therefore, these relations were based on mutual assistance and co-operation. These relations were conditioned by the fact that people with their primitive implements could only withstand the mighty forces of nature together, collectively. In such a situation, exploitation of man by man did not exist because of two reasons. Firstly, the tools used (means of production) were so simple that they could be reproduced by any one. These were implements like spear, stick, bow and arrow etc. Hence no person or group of people had the monopoly of ownership over the tools. Secondly, production was at a low scale. The people existed more or less on a subsistence lord. Their production was just sufficient to meet the needs of the people provided everybody worked. Therefore it was a situation of no master and no servant. All were equal. Gradually, with time man started perfecting his tools, his craft of producing and surplus production started taking place. This led to private property and primitive equality gave way to social inequality. Thus, the first antagonistic classes, slaves and slave owners appeared. This is how the development of the forces of production led to the replacement of primitive communal system by slavery.

2) **Slave-owning:**

In the slave-owning society, primitive tools were perfected and bronze and iron tools replaced the stone and wooden implements. Large scale agriculture, livestock rising, mining and handicrafts developed. The development of this type of forces of production also changed the relations of production. These relations were based on the slave owners absolute ownership of both the means of production and the slave himself and everything he produced. The owner left the slave only with the bare minimum necessities to keep him from dying of starvation. In this system, the history of exploitation of man by man and the history of class struggle began. The development of productive forces went on and slavery became an impediment to the expansion of social production. Production demanded the constant improvement of implements, higher labour productivity but the slave had no interest in this as it would not improve his position. With the passage of time the class conflict between the classes of slave owners and the slaves became acute and it was manifested in slave revolts. These revolts together with the raids from neighbouring tribes undermined the foundations of slavery leading to a new stage, i.e. Feudal system.

3) **Feudal:**

The Progressive development of the productive forces continued under feudalism. Man started using inanimate sources of energy, i.e. water and wind, besides human labour. The crafts advanced further, new implements and machines were invented and old ones are improved. The labour of craftsmen was specialized raising productivity considerably. The development of forces of production led to emergence of feudal relations of production. These relations were based on the feudal lord's ownership of the serfs or landless peasants. The production relations were relations of dominations and subjection, exploitation of the serfs by the feudal lords. Nevertheless, these relations were more progressive than in slavery system, because they made the labourers interested to some extent, in their labour. The peasants and the artisans could own the implements or small parts of land. These forces of production underwent changes due to new discoveries, increasing demands for consumption caused by population increase and discovery of new markets through colonialism. All this led to the need and growth of mass scale manufacture. This became possible due to advances in technology. This brought the unorganized labourers at one place, i.e. the factory. This sparked off already sharpened class conflict leading to peasant revolution against landowners. The new system of production demanded free labourer whereas the serf was tied to the land; therefore the new forces of production also changed the relations of production culminating into a change in the mode of production from feudalism to capitalism.

4) Intensification of Class Conflict under Capitalism:

Large-scale machine production is the specific feature of the productive forces of capitalism. Huge factories, plants and mines took place of artisan workshops and manufactures. In a century or two, capitalism accomplished much more in developing the productive forces than had been done in all the proceeding eras of human history. The vigorous growth of the forces of production was helped by the capitalist relations of production based on private capitalist ownership. Under capitalism, the producer, the proletariat, is legally free, being attached neither to the land nor to any particular factory. They are free in the sense that they can go to work for any capitalist, but they are not free from the bourgeois class as a whole. Possessing no means of production, they are compelled to sell their labour power and thereby came under the yoke of exploitation. Due to this exploitation the relatively free labourers became conscious of their class interest and organize themselves into a working class movement. This working class movement intensified its struggle against the bourgeois class. It begins with bargaining for better wages and working conditions and cultivates into an intensified class conflict which is aimed at over throwing the capitalist system. Marx said that the capitalist system symbolises the most acute form of inequality, exploitation and class antagonism. This paves the way for a socialist revolution which would lead to a new stage of society i.e. Communism.

5) Class Struggle:

The theory of class struggle is central to Marxian thought. The first line of Communist Manifesto (1848) reads: "The history of all hitherto existing society is the history of class struggle." "Freeman and, slave, patricians and plebian, lord and serf, guild master and journey man, in a word, oppressor and the oppressed stood in constant opposition to one another, carried on uninterrupted now hidden and now open fight, a fight that each time ended in a revolutionary reconstitution of society at large, or in common ruin of the contending classes." The perpetual tension, conflict or the antagonism between the owning and the non-owning class is called Class struggle. Not only the classes but also the class struggle is economically conditioned. Therefore Marx says that economic relationship is the very basis of all other types of relationships. i.e., social, political and legal and these are called the super structures. Economic relationship decides, defines and determines all other forms of relationships; i.e. social, political and legal. This is what is called the concept of economic determinism by Marx.

Causes of the Class Struggle:

However, the nature of conflict under the capitalist system is qualitatively different. The exploited have become aware of their exploitation. They have got organised not only within their own country, but all over the world. Thus under capitalism, the struggle between the „bourgeoisie" and the „proletariat" is more intense than in any other previous stages in history. In capitalism, power influence and wealth of the capitalists have increased. Condition of the proletarians has become miserable. The crises will increase. 'The Communist Manifesto" makes an appeal to the proletariat to unite to overthrow the capitalist socio-economic and political order. The Communist Manifesto makes an appeal to the proletariat to unite to overthrow the capitalist socio-economic and political order.

6) Inevitability of Destruction of Capitalism:

According to Marx, Capitalism does contain the seeds of self-destruction. Large-scale production and monopoly are the characteristic features of capitalism. This leads to the concentration of wealth in the hands of fewer persons. The few capitalists become extremely rich. Proletariat are subjected to exploitation and become poorer and poorer. They will feel capitalism is the source of their misery and suffering. The interest of the capitalist class is to maximise the profit, whereas the interest of the working class lies in the enhancement of wage. So tension is created between these two classes. It generates the feeling of class-consciousness among the workers. Finally, when exploitation is heightened to the maximum and the misery and suffering of the industrial workers become unbearable under capitalism. Proletariat will make a joint appeal for a bloody revolution against the capitalists. This is followed by the establishment of the proletariat's dictatorship. According to Marx, the conflict and contradiction is the main source of revolution. Proper consciousness among the workers creates an atmosphere conducive to revolution. Consciousness about their position, about the utility of struggle in this matter Ideology will play the important role. It makes the people conscious.

According to Marx, existence of contradiction and consciousness is very much vital for revolution. People must be mentally prepared to make any sacrifice for the success of revolution. Hence, Marx makes appeal to the workers of the world to unite as they have nothing to lose but their shackles and have a world to win. Thus, Marx with the help of his ideology tried to bring mental preparedness in the workers. He calls them for a programme of revolutionary action.

E) Criticisms on Class Struggle Theory:

1) Marxian theory of class struggle has been put to various criticisms. This theory is having propaganda value. The theory of revolution that Marx presents on the basis of the conflict of interest between the social classes is not convincing. There may be revolution due to causes other than these; and the same may not involve force or violence.
2) The technological revolution of 18th and 19th century, the constitutional changes in the 19th century England, Arya Samaj movement of Dayanand Saraswati are illustrations of the revolutionary changes brought about in the respective areas, without the use of force. The abolition of caste system by the legislative measures is no less revolutionary.
3) Marx has made many predictions in regard to the development of the future capitalistic society especially in regard to its relations with the proletariat and about the inevitable struggle between the capitalist and the proletariat has not come off. Marx has ignored social conditions. He has failed to distinguish between the social and economic classes. It has been said that it is not correct to believe that all struggle is always a class struggle. He has not followed the nature of struggle.
4) The concept of alienation of individual from his social system is a complete ambiguity. Marx sociology reduces him to mere zero. There is however, no change in his position. Karl Marx leaves him as much hand and foot bound in his system, as he found him under the established one. The hope of achieving the total man is thus completely lost.
5) Max Weber considered the philosophy of Marx as “false”; “because it is incompatible with both the nature of science and nature of human existence.” Max Weber does not support that only economic factor can influence the course of history.
6) Marxian concept of classless society remains only as a political instrument in the hands of the communists. This concept is being misused for gaining political benefits. It is thus reduced to the level of a tool of political propoganda. Marxian theory of classless society is a kind of Utopian dream.

Bogardus says, “Marxian communism is the result of the Plato’s communism and Moore’s Utopianism.” In spite of the above criticisms, shortcomings, the theory of the classless society, class and class struggle has, had a tremendous appeal to the people with a sense of social justice.

1.3 Feminist Perspective:

There are quite a few movements across the world, in particular, the western world that project women’s issues with emphasis on creating egalitarian social conditions wherein the ideal of gender equality should be one of the cardinal values. Collectively these movements are known as feminism. The objectives of the feminist movement are broadly similar to those of the campaigns for women’s rights but in recent years it has acquired ideological and theoretical dimensions that have registered an impact on social sciences. In this respect, the notion of a feminist approach to political theory assumes significance. Accordingly, we may say that feminism makes attempts to bring into light an approach to the study of social sciences that helps establish, promote and define social concepts from the point of view of gender egalitarianism rather than the male perspective that has been the case till recently. In order to delineate the feminist approach to political theory it is essential to have a cursory look on the history of feminism and its dynamics.

1.3.1 Gilman Theory of Gender Inequality:

Charlotte Perkins Gilman (1860-1935) is an American intellectual and sociologist who critiqued the idea of gender inequality. Gender inequality is the economic and political disparities due to gender. Economically, there are disparities between wealth and income. Politically, there are disparities between legal rights. Gilman points out that a female's economic position is basically determined by her husband or father (closest male relationship). Women lack economic independence.

1) **Blending of Gender Spheres:**

Throughout time, there has always been a subconscious struggle for gender equality. However, within recent history this struggle has been made conscious. As society progresses, the separate male and female spheres begin to blend. Within this blend, there is another separation: separate spheres in the work force and separate spheres at home. In these two separations, with time, the male and female spheres will again blend.

2) **Gender Inequality in the Home:**

This is the world we live in today. In current society, it is not uncommon to see men and women working alongside each other as equals. Seemingly, this progression would also make a blending transition between male and female partners within the home. Alas, studies have shown that this is not the case.

Today, many male and female spheres remain separated within the household. Why does this inequality persist? Will it be eventually be overcome? As we look at Charlotte Perkins Gilman's novel *Herland*, we begin to see what shapes these spheres.

In the realm of unpaid household labor, gender inequality is still an issue because of the remnants of a male-dominated, patriarchal world, where men dealt with labor and women dealt with motherhood.

3) **Primitive Gender Roles:**

Through my own observations of society, I believe there is gender inequality because of two physiological circumstances: man's innate ability for hard labor, and woman's innate ability to give birth.

Since the beginning of time, men were seen as hunter-gatherers who would provide food for the development of the species, and, similar to the Herlander mind frame, "By motherhood [women] were born and by motherhood [women lived]–life was, [for women], just the long cycle of motherhood".

As a materialistic world developed, the distinctly separate spheres of men and women became less important for the species' survival. Eventually, any type of life became possible for men and women. This is clearly observed in our modern age of women in the workplace and men as stay-at-home fathers. But if spheres have blended, why does inequality persist?

4) A Changing Patriarchal Society:

I believe inequality persists because of the original two innate features of men and women. As man ventured out to get food for the family, the world first became his. Woman, on the other hand, did not venture into the world as man did; thus, the home became hers. As man slowly shaped the world, he did so in reflection of his masculinity.

In *Herland*, Vandyck Jennings was led to the conviction that "'feminine charms' [men] are so fond of are not feminine at all, but mere reflected masculinity–developed to please [men] because [women] had to please [men]". A masculine world created patriarchy.

From the very beginning of society, women were subjected to a male view of life; they constantly had to struggle when striving for an equal playing ground in a male oriented world.

Now, women have caught up. Technological advances put men and women at the same level. The male and female spheres have blended in all places but one: the home. Will gender inequality ever be overcome within the home? Yes.

I believe that soon, men and women spheres will blend in the home as well. As society continues to progress, women will slowly lose the old ideals of womanhood and servitude. The reason men treat women unequally within the home is because of their mothers.

Men's mothers still held many of the separate sphere ideals that result in men being constantly treated for by women within the home. Soon, as old mothers are forgotten and next generations of mothers bloom, women will hold little remembrance of servitude for men. Separate spheres will once again blend, and women will gain equal ground not only in the workplace, but in the home as well.

5) Relearning Gender Roles and Identity:

Similarly, in *Herland*, Gilman portrays just how different male and female spheres used to be. Within the novel, the separate spheres are described in extremes. The spheres move beyond gender, and become two distinctly separated societies: patriarchal and matriarchal.

At first the men could not understand the subtle differences of how the women of *Herland* were apt to think. "There was no accepted standard of what was 'manly' and was 'womanly'".

Originally, the men lived within patriarchal conventions, but as instances such as Jeff's conversation with Celis arose, the men began to see their firm ideas of a superior patriarchal society dwindle. "'A woman should not have to carry anything,' Celis said, 'Why?' [Jeff] could not look that fleet-footed, deep-chested young forester in the face and say, 'Because she is weaker.' She wasn't".

The difficulty the patriarch-minded men had with the matriarch-minded women understood that in *Herland*, there were no inequalities. The men, coming from a socially divided world, often times saw no fault in their mind frame until a common sensed matriarchal-thought presented itself.

During Terry, Jeff, and Zava's conversation about virginity, these gender driven views were presented of how divided the social ideals of a patriarchal society can be. "'The term *virgin* is applied to the female who has not mated,' [Jeff] answered. 'Oh, I see. And does it apply to the male also?'. . . He passed this over rather hurriedly. . .".

As Gilman further expresses her thoughts on gender inequality through the characters of Herland, separate spheres within closer relationships becomes more prominent.

6) Coming to a Common Understanding:

While the men's view on life slowly changed, such as Jeff seeing Celis' point about women being equal in the workplace, it seemed that the patriarchal and matriarchal spheres began to blend. Near the end of the novel, the final struggle between gender driven spheres takes places within marriage.

The men were feeling inadequate within the matriarchal society. "Here we were penniless guests and strangers, with no chance even to use our strength and courage–nothing to defend them from or protect them against". With nothing left to give, the men attempt to give the Herlanders their last names.

This seems idiotic to do within a society where last names were seldom used, but at this point the men were desperate and needed to make their mark. "'What makes us all feel foolish,' I told the girls, 'is that her we have nothing to give you–except, of course our names" .

In the end of *Herland*, Gilman describes gender inequality as something that only arises from the patriarchal society's mind frame. Even though Val tried his best to get "Ellador's point of view, and naturally [he] tried to give her [his]," the main problems came from thoughts of superiority within a close relationship of marriage: "Of course, what we, as men, wanted to make them see was that there were other, and as we proudly said 'higher,' uses in this relation than what Terry called 'mere parentage".

Perhaps the patriarchal views blending into the Herlander views are not so different from the blended views within marriage today. Both sides of the sphere would like to make their stand within the relationship, but also, both sides will eventually understand each other.

When these spheres blend within the home, just as we have already seen in the workforce, then I, just as Gilman too suggested, will have considered human development to have overcome another obstacle in our unequally driven history.

7) The Abolition of Gender Roles:

In conclusion, as inequality within the workplace has seemingly been overcome, separate gender spheres within the domesticated home still remain a problem in *Herland*. However, as male and female spheres continue to slowly blend with each other, I predict that within the next few generations, gender inequality between marriage partners will become obsolete.

Just as Gilman suggested, the main problems arose from the male-oriented views of how society should be run. Since males ventured into the world first, this view seems only natural. As women move up the social ladder, they continue to make their mark in a patriarchal society. Soon our unequally driven history will come to an end.

****

Review Questions

Q.1 Answers in 100 Words:

1) Explain the Structural-Functional Perspective.
2) Write Short Note on Conflict Perspective.
3) Discuss in Short about Feminist Perspective.
4) State the Criticism of the AGIL Scheme.
5) Explain the Concept of Class Struggle.

Q.2 Answers in 200 Words:

1) Explain the Systematic Depiction of AGIL Functions.
2) State the Classification of Societies in History and Emergence of Classes.
3) State the Criticisms on Class Struggle Theory.

Q.3 Answers in 300 Words:

1) Explain in detail about the Talcott Parson's AGIL Model.
2) Discuss in detail about the Karl Marx's Theory of Class Struggle.
3) Explain the Gilman Theory of Gender Inequality.

Q.4 Write Short Note on Following:

1) Concept of Class Struggle.
2) Criticism of the AGIL Scheme.
3) Criticisms on Class Struggle Theory.
4) Gilman Theory of Gender Inequality.

****

UNIT 2

Social Stratification & Mobility

2.1 Social Stratification

2.2 Social Mobility

Introduction:

The main difference between social stratification and social mobility is that social stratification is the way people are ranked and ordered in society, while social mobility is the movement of individuals through a system of social stratification. Every society has a system of stratification; society categorizes people into different ranks and positions according to various factors. For example, the society we live in today uses a stratification system based on income and wealth. Sometimes, it is also possible to move through the strata in social stratification and reach a different level. We call this ability to move through social stratification social mobility. The world around us consists of human beings divided into different social segments based on caste, ethnic and racial attributes on the one hand and social strata, status groups and social classes based on economic and political dimensions of the individual and the groups on the other. Based on these criteria there exist inequalities among human beings terms of rulers and the subjects, rich and poor, elite and commoner and so on. While segmental divisions are based on non-economic factors, the social strata and dashes come into being on the basis of economic and political positions occupied by the individuals or their group in the social structure of the society. All this exist despite all religions since time immemorial and the constitutions of almost all the countries ever since their implementation all over the world have been proclaiming equality among all irrespective of caste, creed, sex, colour and religion.

2.1 Social Stratification:

Stratification refers to systematic social inequality in the access of opportunities, resources, and rewards. It involves the uneven distribution of people across social categories based upon achieved and ascribed characteristics. Human societies differ greatly in the extent of stratification present within them. Social stratification refers to the division of individuals in different groups, categories, strata or layers based on social differences like income, power. Wealth and status and biological differences like gender and ethnicity. This follows that class inequalities, gender inequalities and ethnic inequalities reflect the various forms of divisions or stratifications that exist in society. There has never been an equal society. People have always known some form of social stratification.

2.1.1 Meaning:

Social stratification is a particular form of social inequality. All societies arrange their members in terms of superiority, inferiority and equality. Stratification is a process of interaction or differentiation whereby some people come to rank higher than others. In one word, when individuals and groups are ranked, according to some commonly accepted basis of valuation in a hierarchy of status levels based upon the inequality of social positions, social stratification occurs. Social stratification means division of society into different strata or layers. It involves a hierarchy of social groups. Members of a particular layer have a common identity. They have a similar life style.

2.1.2 Definitions:

Following are the definitions of social stratification:

1) **Ogburn and Nimkoff :**

   "The process by which individuals and groups are ranked in more or less enduring hierarchy of status is known as stratification"

2) **Lundberg :**

   "A stratified society is one marked by inequality, by differences among people that are evaluated by them as being lower and higher.

3) **Gisbert :**

   "Social stratification is the division of society into permanent groups of categories linked with each other by the relationship of superiority and subordinations".

4) **Williams :**

   "Social Stratification refers to "The ranking of individuals on a scale of superiority-inferiority equality, according to some commonly accepted basis of valuation."

2.1.3 Characteristics of Social Stratification :

On the basis of the analysis of the different definitions given by eminent scholars, social stratification may have the following characteristics.

1) **Social Stratification is Universal :**

   There is no society on this world which is free from stratification. Modern stratification differs from stratification of primitive societies. It is a worldwide phenomenon. According to Sorokin "all permanently organised groups are stratified."

2) Stratification is Social:

It is true that biological qualities do not determine one's superiority and inferiority. Factors like age, sex, intelligence as well as strength often contribute as the basis on which statues are distinguished. But one's education, property, power, experience, character, personality etc. are found to be more important than biological qualities. Hence, stratification is social by nature.

3) It is Ancient:

Stratification system is very old. It was present even in the small wondering bonds. In almost all the ancient civilisations, the differences between the rich and poor, humble and powerful existed. During the period of Plato and Kautilya even emphasis was given to political, social and economic inequalities.

4) It is in Diverse Forms:

The forms of stratification are not uniform in all the societies. In the modern world class, caste and estate are the general forms of stratification. In India a special type of stratification in the form of caste is found. The ancient Aryas were divided into four varnas: the Brahmins, Kshatriyas, Vaishyas and Sudras. The ancient Greeks were divided into freemen and slaves and the ancient Romans were divided into the patricians and the plebians. So every society, past or present, big or small is characterised by diversed forms of social stratification.

5) Social Stratification is Consequential:

Social stratification has two important consequences one is "life chances" and the other one is "life style". A class system not only affects the "life- chances" of the individuals but also their "life style". The members of a class have similar social chances but the social chances vary in every society. It includes chances of survival and of good physical and mental health, opportunities for education, chances of obtaining justice, marital conflict, separation and divorce etc. Life style denotes a style of life which is distinctive of a particular social status. Life-styles include such matters like the residential areas in every community which have gradations of prestige ranking, mode of housing, means of recreation, the kinds of dress, the kinds of books; TV shows to which one is exposed and so on. Life-style may be viewed as a sub-culture in which one stratum differs from another within the frame work of a commonly shared over-all culture.

2.1.4 Forms of Stratification:

Social stratification has been analyzed by different scholars from different points of view.

Stratification structures may take different forms. Sociologist Max Weber distinguishes between class, status and party. Similarly T.B. Bottom ore has distinguished four types or forms of stratification such as slavery, Estate, Caste and Class. These forms are:

1) **Cast:**

Caste is another important form of stratification. It is a closed form of stratification. Caste is both a structural and cultural phenomenon. Caste system is one of the most important forms of stratification system in India. The term caste has been derived from the Portuguese word 'casta' which means breed, race or kind. Caste is an endogamous hereditary group based on the notion of purity and pollution. An individual is born with fixed status which cannot be changed during his life time. It expresses a hierarchical relationship. Individual achievements cannot change ones' caste. People at the top of the hierarchy are given highest place and people at the bottom of the hierarchy enjoy lowest status. Caste system is the basis of Hindu social organization. Occupation and restrictions on food, drink and social intercourse are associated with caste system. Social mobility is restricted within caste system. Hindu society was divided into four varnas namely, Brahmin, Kshatriya, Vaishya and Sudra. While the Brahmins enjoy top rank the Sudras enjoy lowest rank in the caste hierarchy. Varnas are found throughout India but caste groups are local or regional. In the traditional Indian villages caste system provided the mechanism for the exchange of goods and services through Jajmani system which is an expression of interdependence among castes.

2) **Class:**

Class is another important modern form of stratification. Its' basis is economic. It is an open system of stratification. Classes are characteristics of industrial societies. Class is a factual structure without any religious or legal sanction. Classes are groups who are ranked on the basis of specific criteria. They are social groups which occupy specific position in a given society. A class is made up of people of similar social status who regard one another as social equals. Each class is a subculture, with a set of attitudes, beliefs, values and behaviour norms which differ from those of other classes. Classes are stratified according to their relation to the factors of production and acquisition of goods. Classes are distinguished on the basis of a distinct life style. Class status is determined by property, achievement and skill of an individual. Persons engaged in similar occupation, having equal economic status and similar life style belong to the same class. Members of a class have common economic interests and class consciousness. Thus, a social class consists of those groups of people who share similar opportunities, similar life style, similar economic status in society and live in similar class situation. Marx defined class in economic terms whereas Max Weber considers class as a status group who share similar life chances.

3) **Gender:**

The most common explanation for divisions between men and women is that the male 'sex' is stronger, more intelligent and more of a 'natural' leader. Women however according to biological determinism are generally seen as child bearers and instinctively house keepers. Although this is widely considered a biological point of view, sociologists like Talcott Parsons (1959) have tended to lean towards this idea. In addition to age, gender is one of the universal dimensions on which status differences are based. Unlike sex, which is a biological concept, gender is a social construct specifying the socially and culturally prescribed roles that men and women are to follow. According to Gerda Lerner in The Creation of Patriarchy, gender is the "costume, a mask, a straitjacket in which men and women dance their unequal dance" (p.238). As Alan Wolfe observed in "The Gender Question" (The New Republic, June 6:27-34), "of all the ways that one group has systematically mistreated another, none is more deeply rooted than the way men have subordinated women. All other discriminations pale by contrast." Lerner argues that the subordination of women preceded all other subordinations and that to rid ourselves of all of those other "isms"--racism, classism, ageism, etc.it is sexism that must first be eradicated.

Socialisation is the most important process in a person's life, permitting the development of an individual's social capacities, as well as learning norms and values that permit adequate participation in society. During this process, the family is one of the most important social environments, in that it permits the connection with the social structure. To a large extent, a child's development possibilities depend on his/her family's characteristics and socio-economic position in society. Socialisation also implies social differentiation, as it prepares boys and girls to be part of a specific social group.

The socialisation process is crucial for the internalisation of the social and cultural reality. The process is also highly charged with emotions: boys and girls identify with these realities, which determine what contents and aspects they consider important enough to be part of their own norms, values and lives. The process of primary socialisation goes beyond a merely cognitive learning process and remains firmly rooted in the conscience of girls and boys – to a much greater extent than any subsequent secondary socialisations. Gender role socialisation is carried on by parents who choose blue for boys and pink for girls. Blue is a cold colour whereas pink is warm and these colours are used for cards, clothing and even maternity ward tags. Boys are taught to be leaders, strong, active, dominating, and never showing weakness. Girls on the other hand are taught to be caring, looked after and to be good-natured and well-mannered. As girls become women they are socialised into roles such as a wife and mother and taught that it is a desirable life choice to settle down. This leads to women not having access to as many life chances as men, and being reliant on the opposite sex for income, all attributes that lead to less independence for women. Even when women do dispel these gender roles and seek to become more independent they often face employers that do not share the same views. It is common for the employer to assume that a female employee will want to take leave to have children, and even though there are laws that prohibit employers asking such questions during interviews, this doesn't stop this being a common view.

Education is different from other forms of socialisation such as family because it involves an instruction that is deliberate expression of a formal institution. Institutions promote the values of the dominant culture. There is probably less variation in what children learn from schooling than what they learn as a result of informal interactions with the family or friends. For non-white people, family and cultural identity is seen as a necessary tool to counteract the effects of an institution actively promotes and sustains an unequal position when compared to their white counterparts. There is some support for this position in "Introductory sociology" which states that the 1944 Education Act was designed to allow fair access to schooling for not only boys but also girls. There were two reasons for widening access to education by the Government.

4) **Ethnicity:**

We sometimes confuse race and ethnicity, but these are different. Ethnicity refers to shared membership in a cultural group. Like race, it is also socially constructed. But, like race, ethnicity also has major consequences for people's life chances. We tend to think of ethnic minorities as inferior, which are what results in a system of ethnic stratification. Ethnic minorities in our society are much less likely than whites to obtain an advanced degree, like the black population. Income and wealth are also stratified along ethnic lines. For example, Hispanics have more accumulated wealth than blacks, but less wealth than whites.

5) **Age:**

In sociology, age stratification refers to the hierarchical ranking of people into age groups within a society. Age stratification could also be defined as a system of inequalities linked to age. In Western societies, for example, both the old and the young are perceived and treated as relatively incompetent and excluded from much social life. Age stratification based on an ascribed status is a major source inequality, and thus may lead to ageism. Ageism is a social inequality resulting from age stratification. This is a sociological concept that comes with studying aging population. Age stratification within a population can have major implications, affecting things such as workforce trends, social norms, family structures, government policies, and even health outcomes.

6) **Power:**

The second basis of social stratification is power, or the capacity to influence people and events to obtain wealth and prestige. That is, having power is positively correlated with being rich, as evidenced by the domination of wealthy males in high-ranking governmental positions. Wealthier Americans are also more likely to be politically active as way of ensuring their continued power and wealth. In contrast, poorer Americans are less likely to be politically active, given their sense of powerlessness to influence the process.

Because wealth is distributed unequally, the same is clearly true of power. Elite theorists argue that a few hundred individuals hold all of the power in the United States. These power elite, who may come from similar backgrounds and have similar interests and values, hold key positions in the highest branches of the government, military, and business world. Conflict theorists hold that only a small number of Americans the capitalists hold the vast majority of power in the United States. They may not actually hold political office, but they nonetheless influence politics and governmental policies for their own benefit and to protect their interests. An example is the large corporation that tries to limit the amount of fees it must pay through political contributions that ultimately put certain people into office who then sway policy decisions.

On the other hand, pluralist theorists hold that power is not in the hands of the elite or a few, but rather it is widely distributed among assorted competing and diverse groups. In other words, unlike elitists and Marxists, pluralists note little if any inequality in the distribution of power. For instance, citizens can influence political outcomes by voting candidates into or out of office. And the power of labor groups is balanced by the power of businesses, which is balanced by the power of the government. In a democracy, no one is completely powerless.

2.1.5 Perspective on Stratification:

Social stratification takes on new meanings when it is examined from different sociological perspectives - functionalism, conflict theory, and symbolic interactionism.

1) **Functionalism:**

In sociology, the functionalist perspective examines how society's parts operate. According to functionalism, different aspects of society exist because they serve a needed purpose. What is the function of social stratification?

In 1945, sociologists Kingsley Davis and Wilbert Moore published the Davis-Moore thesis, which argued that the greater the functional importance of a social role, the greater must be the reward. The theory posits that social stratification represents the inherently unequal value of different work. Certain tasks in society are more valuable than others. Qualified people who fill those positions must be rewarded more than others.

According to Davis and Moore, a firefighter's job is more important than, for instance, a grocery store cashiers. The cashier position does not require the same skill and training level as firefighting. Without the incentive of higher pay and better benefits, why would someone be willing to rush into burning buildings? If pay levels were the same, the firefighter might as well work as a grocery store cashier. Davis and Moore believed that rewarding more important work with higher levels of income, prestige, and power encourages people to work harder and longer.

Davis and Moore stated that, in most cases, the degree of skill required for a job determines that job's importance. They also stated that the more skill required for a job, the fewer qualified people there would be to do that job. Certain jobs, such as cleaning hallways or answering phones, do not require much skill. The employees don't need a college degree. Other work, like designing a highway system or delivering a baby, requires immense skill.

In 1953, Melvin Tumin countered the Davis-Moore thesis in "Some Principles of Stratification: A Critical Analysis." Tumin questioned what determined a job's degree of importance. The Davis-Moore thesis does not explain, he argued, why a media personality with little education, skill, or talent becomes famous and rich on a reality show or a campaign trail. The thesis also does not explain inequalities in the education system or inequalities due to race or gender. Tumin believed social stratification prevented qualified people from attempting to fill roles (Tumin 1953). For example, an underprivileged youth has less chance of becoming a scientist, no matter how smart she is, because of the relative lack of opportunity available to her. The Davis-Moore thesis also does not explain why a basketball player earns millions of dollars a year when a doctor who saves lives, a soldier who fights for others' rights and a teacher who helps form the minds of tomorrow will likely not make millions over the course of their careers.

The Davis-Moore thesis, though open for debate, was an early attempt to explain why stratification exists. The thesis states that social stratification is necessary to promote excellence, productivity, and efficiency, thus giving people something to strive for. Davis and Moore believed that the system serves society as a whole because it allows everyone to benefit to a certain extent.

2) Conflict Theory:

These people are protesting a decision made by Tennessee Technological University in Cookeville, Tennessee, to lay off custodians and outsource the jobs to a private firm to avoid paying employee benefits. Private Job agencies often pay lower hourly wages. Is the decision fair?

Conflict theorists are deeply critical of social stratification, asserting that it benefits only some people, not all of society. For instance, to a conflict theorist, it seems wrong that a basketball player is paid millions for an annual contract while a public school teacher earns $35,000 a year. Stratification, conflict theorists believe, perpetuates inequality. Conflict theorists try to bring awareness to inequalities, such as how a rich society can have so many poor members.

Many conflict theorists draw on the work of Karl Marx. During the nineteenth-century era of industrialization, Marx believed social stratification resulted from people's relationship to production. People were divided by a single line: they either owned factories or worked in them. In Marx's time, bourgeois capitalists owned high-producing businesses, factories, and land, as they still do today. Proletariats were the workers who performed the manual labor to produce goods. Upper-class capitalists raked in profits and got rich, while working-class proletariats earned skimpy wages and struggled to survive. With such opposing interests, the two groups were divided by differences of wealth and power. Marx saw workers experience deep alienation, isolation and misery resulting from powerless status levels (Marx 1848). Marx argued that proletariats were oppressed by the money-hungry bourgeois.

Today, while working conditions have improved, conflict theorists believe that the strained working relationship between employers and employees still exists. Capitalists own the means of production, and a system is in place to make business owners rich and keep workers poor. According to conflict theorists, the resulting stratification creates class conflict. If he were alive in today's economy, as it recovers from a prolonged recession, Marx would likely have argued that the recession resulted from the greed of capitalists, satisfied at the expense of working people.

3) **Symbolic Interactionism:**

Symbolic interactionism is a theory that uses everyday interactions of individuals to explain society as a whole. Symbolic interactionism examines stratification from a micro-level perspective. This analysis strives to explain how people's social standing affects their everyday interactions.

In most communities, people interact primarily with others who share the same social standing. It is precisely because of social stratification that people tend to live, work, and associate with others like themselves, people who share their same income level, educational background, or racial background, and even tastes in food, music, and clothing. The built-in system of social stratification groups people together. This is one of the reasons why it was rare for a royal prince like England's Prince William to marry a commoner.

Symbolic interactionists also note that people's appearance reflects their perceived social standing. Housing, clothing, and transportation indicate social status, as do hairstyles, taste in accessories, and personal style.

2.2 Social Mobility:

Individuals are recognized in society through the statuses they occupy and the roles they enact. The society as well as individuals is dynamic. Men are normally engaged in endless endeavor to enhance their statuses in society, move from lower position to higher position, secure superior job from an inferior one. For various reasons people of the higher status and position may be forced to come down to a lower status and position. Thus people in society continue to move up and down the status scale. This movement is called social mobility.

2.2.1 Meaning:

Mobility stands for shift, change and movement. The change may be of a place or from one position to another. Further, change is value free i.e. it cannot be said that change is for good or bad. When we prefix 'social' along with mobility it would imply that people or individual occupying a social position, move to another position or status. In the social ladder this movement may be upward or downward or it may be inter-generational or intra-generational. In short, social mobility stands for change in the position of an individual or a group of individuals from one status to another.

2.2.2 Definitions:

Following are the definitions of social mobility:

1) **Barber:**

   "Social mobility refers to movement, either upward or downward between higher or lowers social classes; or more precisely, movement between one relatively full time, functionally significant social role and another that is evaluated as either higher or lower."

2) **Wallace and Wallace:**

   "Social mobility is the movement of a person or persons from one social status to another. W.P Scott has defined sociology as the movement of an individual or group from one social class or social stratum to another."

2.2.3 Forms of Social Mobility:

Change of social position of an individual or group of individuals takes different forms and shapes. At one period of time there would be one type of mobility and another period of time it can be another type. Each of the following types is not exclusive but they may overlap, it is only for the purpose of convenience and analysis they are given different labels.

1) **Horizontal Mobility:**

   Under this type of social mobility, a person changes his or her occupation but the overall social standing remains the same. Certain occupations like Doctor, Engineer, and Professor may enjoy the same status but when an engineer changes his occupation from engineer to teaching engineering, he has horizontally moved from one occupational category to another. But no change has taken place in the system of social stratification.

In other words, horizontal mobility is the transition of an individual or social object from one social group to another situated on the same level. While explaining horizontal mobility we are mainly referring to movement of individuals from one position to another of more or less equal prestige. Sorokin explains the concept of horizontal mobility still more broadly.

According to Sorokin, "Horizontal mobility refers to territorial, religious, political party, family, occupational and other horizontal shifting without any noticeable change in vertical position." An increase of territorial circulation of individuals within Western societies since the second half of the nineteenth century indicates horizontal mobility. The individuals are no more attached to their place of birth. The individuals move from one place to another in search of jobs which may be of same prestige. The modern means of transportation have brought in more territorial movement of individuals. The other expression of territorial mobility, according to Sorokin, is greater circulation of social things and values which refer to newspaper news, automobile implements, birth control or money, if social thing is used by more and more people of the same class, regardless of the country or territorial boundaries, then this is an example of horizontal expression.

In addition to this, the shifting of individuals from one job or factory or occupation' to another of the same kind refers to horizontal circulation especially, if they do not represent any noticeable change in vertical direction. These kinds of intra-occupational circulation or labour turnover, therefore, refer to not only vertical but horizontal intra-occupational mobility. Sorokin further indicates that since territorial, family, intra-occupational mobility of present Western society is intensive it is expected to be accompanied by a considerably horizontal circulation of the individuals from State to State, from one religious group to another, from one political party to another and generally from one ideological group to another.

2) Vertical Mobility:

Vertical mobility refers to any change in the occupational, economic or political status of an individual or a group which leads to change of their position. In the words of Sorokin, by vertical social mobility is meant the relations involved in transition of an individual (or a social object) from one social stratum to another. According to the direction of transition, there are two types of vertical social mobility – ascending and descending or social climbing and social sinking. The ascending currents exist in the two principal forms – as an infiltration of the individuals of a lower stratum into an existing higher one, and as a creation of such a group into a higher stratum instead of, or side by side, with the existing group of this stratum.

In simple words, vertical mobility stands for change of social position either upward or downward, which can be labelled as ascending or descending type of mobility. When a big businessman meets with losses in his business and is declared bankrupt, he occupies a low status. On the other hand, if a small businessman with occupational skills of money and manipulation becomes an industrialist he occupies a higher position in the social ladder. Hence his position improves in the hierarchical order.

Principles of Vertical Mobility:

Vertical mobility is intensive in relatively open societies. Sorokin has indicated the following general principles of vertical mobility:

a) There has scarcely been any society whose strata were absolutely closed or in which vertical mobility in its three forms – economic, political and occupational was not present.

b) There has never been existed a society in which vertical social mobility has been absolutely free and the transition from one social stratum to another has had no resistance.

c) The intensiveness as well as the generality of vertical social mobility, varies from society to society.

d) The intensiveness and generality of the vertical mobility – the economic, the political and the occupational- fluctuate in the same society at different lines.

3) **Upward Mobility:**

When a person or a group of persons move from lower position to upper position it is called Upward Mobility e.g. a person belonging to a lower caste and occupying a lower position after winning elections becomes a Minister and occupies a higher position. He may not be able to change his caste but with his economic and political power he may move upward. For example, Yadavs in India stand as a testimony to this fact. For the individuals involved, there are many social and psychic costs of upward mobility. Some of the costs are obvious, as men and women break under the strain of a consistent drive for 'success'. In the course of his upward movement, the mobile man must leave behind many people and places. He must leave the ways of thinking and behaving that characterized many of his earlier associations and he must learn, if he can, new ways of thinking and behaving appropriate to his new status.

4) **Downward Mobility:**

Downward mobility indicates that one loses his higher position and occupies a lower position. We can take the example of an individual, who is an Engineer and occupies a respectable position in the society because of his occupational position, education and may be caste. If he is caught for accepting bribe or has committed a sin or has done something wrong, he may be sentenced to jail or members of his caste may outcaste him and as a criminal or as an outcaste he may occupy a lower position vis-a-vis position he was occupying earlier. Under the traditional Indian system if a lady of higher Brahmin caste married a man of Sudra caste, not only the man and woman were out casted but their children were declared as 'chandals.'

Downward Mobility is more stressful for persons who suffer a drastic decline in station position. Men who enjoy orderly -and consistent career tend to make a stable personal, family and community adjustment. Men who are unable to do so are more vulnerable to the most extreme form of personal disorganization – namely suicide. The Downward Mobility is an indicator of the extent to which a society institutionalizes the value of equal opportunity through the creation of structure which supports and facilitates it. Lipset and Zetterberg are of the opinion that this type of mobility is due to interchange of ranks i.e. mobility arising from implementation of equality of opportunity.

5) Inter-Generational Mobility:

This type of mobility means that one generation changes its social status in contrast to preceding generation. However, this mobility may be upward or downward e.g. people of lower caste or class may provide facilities to their children to get higher education, training and skills. With the help of these skills the younger generation may get employment in higher position. If the father is a shoemaker but his son after acquiring education becomes a clerk or a doctor or an engineer, this would be called upward inter- generational mobility. Similarly, a family of Brahmins may be engaged on traditional occupation of teaching and performing rituals but its younger generation is neither intelligent nor follows the family occupation. They become daily wagers then the younger generation has downward inter-generational mobility. With the improvement in economic position, people start changing their style of living by discarding the old practices and adopting the practices of those who are high in social ladder. After two or three generations their new position may be recognized. This process of social mobility, according to Srinivas is a process of Sanskritizon.

Conditions for Inter-generational Mobility:

According to Sorokin, the following conditions affect rates of mobility between generations:

a) Differences between Parents and Offspring's:

If a parent occupies an important position requiring high capacity, his children who are less capable are likely to be downward mobile. Conversely, children who are more capable than their parents are likely to be upwardly mobile, especially open-class societies.

b) Population Change:

In developed and developing countries, greater population expansion at the lower than at the higher levels contribute to upward mobility. Overall population growth creates new positions in the upper and middle levels, where growth is not great enough to fill the vacancies.

c) Changes in Occupational Structure:

With the changing times many occupations have been upgraded and downgraded because their socially defined importance has changed. Some occupations have moved up or down because of changes in the scarcity of workers willing and able to perform their tasks. Such changes in occupational structure have also effected the rates of mobility between generations.

6) **Intra-Generational Mobility:**
This type of mobility takes place in life span of one generation. This can be further divided into two:

a) Change in the position of one individual in his life span

b) Change in the position of one brother but no change in the position of another brother. A person may start his career as a clerk. He acquires more education and skills. Over a period of time, he becomes an IAS officer or a Professor. In this way he moves up and occupies a higher social position than the one with which he had started his career. His brother may have also started his career as a clerk but did not occupy higher position in his life span and continued to remain at the same position. Hence, within the same generation we find that one brother changes his position and other brother does not.

7) **Occupational Mobility:**
Occupational mobility means change from one occupation to another. Different occupations' are hierarchically arranged because the incumbent of these occupations gets different economic rewards and enjoys different power, prestige and privileges based on the economic returns, authority and prestige. These occupations are stratified or hierarchically arranged. When a person or a group of persons move from occupations of lower prestige to occupations of higher prestige, this is called Upward Vertical Mobility. Similarly if an individual or a group of individuals from occupations of higher prestige take up occupations of lower prestige, then this occupational mobility is called Downward Vertical Mobility. From a clerk to an officer is upward vertical occupational mobility; from a clerk to a peon or a smuggler is downward vertical occupational mobility. We must keep in mind that society grants recognition, prestige and power not only based on economic returns from an occupation or profession but according to the skills of the individual which are valued most in the society. A smuggler may be earning more than a clerk but his means of livelihood are not recognized in the society.

Hence, he is placed lower in the social ladder. Now-a-days politicians with their political power occupy higher position irrespective of the means adopted. Hence, people aspire to occupy positions. Occupational mobility, in short, stands for change of occupation of lower prestige to higher and vice-versa. The above noted forms of mobility are not comprehensive and do not include other types of mobility like accretive status achieved and vice-versa or spatial mobility or mobility under caste system. However, the above forms explain the major trends of mobility i.e. upward or downward, vertical and horizontal. Mobility has to be seen in temporal sense i.e. over a period of time. We cannot think of mobility in the absence of time and space.

There are many factors which facilitate social mobility. These factors may be attributed to individual motivation and efforts to improve or the institutions may work out new mechanism or the society at large may bring about drastic changes in the system of evaluation. Let us take these factors individually to find out how they help in social mobility.

2.2.4 Factors Responsible for Social Mobility:

The following factors facilitate Social Mobility:

1) Motivation:

Each individual has a desire not only to have a better way of living but also wants to improve upon his social stand. In open system it is possible to achieve any status. This openness motivates people to work hard and improve upon the skills so that one can attain higher social status. Without such motivation and efforts on the part of the individual social mobility is impossible.

2) Achievements and Failures:

Achievement here refers to extra ordinary, usually unexpected performance, which attracts the attention of a wider public to the abilities of a person. Not all achievements will result in social mobility. Achievements affect status only if they are remarkable. For example, a poor man who has acquired wealth or an unknown writer who has won a literary prize will improve his status. Failures and misdeeds have a similar effect on downward mobility. Fraudulent bankruptcy will remove a member of the upper classes from blue books; he will receive no dinner invitations from his peers and he will become ineligible as a marriage partner. If he is already married, his wife may divorce him. He will have to resign from his clubs and all positions he holds. But he will not become a member of the lowest stratum, although it will be difficult for him to find new association.

3) Education:

Education not only helps an individual to acquire knowledge but is also a passport for occupational position for higher prestige. To become a doctor one has to have education in science subjects. Similarly, to appear in a competitive examination of I.A.S., one has to be at least graduate. It is only after acquiring minimum formal education that individual can aspire to occupy higher positions. It is through education that in modern India the members of Scheduled Castes and Scheduled Tribes are not only able to change their traditional occupation but have also started occupying jobs of higher prestige. In the modern industrial society in which statuses can be achieved, education is basic requirement.

4) Skills and Training:

Each society makes provision to impart skill and training to the younger generation. To acquire skill and training one has to spend a lot of time as well as money. Why these persons spend money and time? The reason being that society gives incentives to such persons. When they complete their training, they are entitled to high positions, which are far better than those positions which they might have taken without such training. Society not only assigns higher social status but also gives higher economic rewards and other privileges to those persons who have these training. Keeping in view these incentives people undergo these training with a hope to move up in the social ladder. In other words, skills and training facilitate in improvement of the position, this leading to social mobility.

5) Migration:

Migration also facilitates social mobility. People migrate from one place to another either due to pull or push factors. A particular place may not have opportunities and facilities to improve upon. Hence, people are forced to migrate to other places to earn their livelihood. At new places, where they migrate, may have different openings and opportunities. These persons avail of these opportunities and improve upon their social position. We can take the example of people belonging to the Scheduled Castes of Uttar Pradesh and Bihar, who migrate to the States of Punjab and Haryana to earn their livelihood. Here they become farm labourers. After acquiring accumulating money they go back to their villages and buy land. They till their own land and become owner cultivators. Hence, from traditional work of Chamars or scavengers, they improve their status and become owner cultivators. Similar is the situation with regard to Asians who migrate to various European countries and the United State of America.

The pull factors attract the people because they do not have those facilities at their place of residence and the new place attracts them by providing these facilities, so that after acquiring new skills and knowledge they could occupy better positions.

People migrate from villages to cities because urban centres have institutions of higher status as well as opportunities for jobs. People come to urban areas to acquire education and skills and occupy higher positions than their parents and brothers who continue to live in villages. In this way we find that both push and pull factors lead to migration which subsequently facilitates social mobility.

6) Industrialization:

Industrial Revolution ushered in a new social system in which people are given status according to their ability and training. No importance was given to their caste, race, religion and ethnicity. Industrialization resulted in mass production at cheaper rate. This forced the artisans out of their work. In search of jobs they migrated to industrial towns. They acquired new vocational training and got jobs in industries. With experience and training they moved up in the social ladder. In the industrial society, the statuses are achieved, whereas in the traditional society like India, the statuses are ascribed according to birth. Hence industrialization facilitates greater social mobility.

7) Urbanization:

In the cities there are more people, they have formal relations. People do not know each other intimately. Urban centres are marked by anonymity. People are close to their friends and relatives only. Urban settlements provide secrecy to individual's caste and background. Individual's position is largely dependent upon his education, occupation and income rather than his background. If an individual has higher education, income and is engaged in occupation of higher prestige, he occupies high social status irrespective of his caste. Urbanization facilitates social mobility by removing those factors which hinder social mobility.

8) Legislation:

The enactment of new laws can also facilitate social mobility. When Zamindari Abolition Act was passed, most of the tenant cultivators became owner cultivators which indicate improvement in their status i.e. from tenants to owner cultivators. Similarly, the legal provision for reservation of jobs and promotion for the Scheduled Castes and Scheduled Tribes has also helped in social mobility. Reservation with regard to admission in professional colleges, job reservation and promotions have a large number of individuals from Scheduled Castes and Scheduled Tribes to improve upon their status. When V.R Singh Government accepted the Mandal Commission report it provided job reservation for the other Backward Classes (OBCs) also. Similarly, the judicial system by passing certain judgments may also facilitate social mobility. Hindu Marriage Act in different ways has enhanced the status of women. Similarly, Hindu Succession Act has given equal rights to the daughter in the family property. Racial Anti-Discrimination Act of America has facilitated social mobility of persons of Black race as well as women. In this way we find that legal provisions also facilitate social mobility.

9) Politicisation:

With education and greater exposure to mass media of communication as well as greater contacts have made people aware about their rights. The political parties also educate the people about their rights. To achieve their rights people unite and force the authority in power to accept their demands. These persons may use agitations, strikes etc. as methods of attaining the desired goals. The political party to get votes provides a number of concessions. With the help of these new concessions and provisions, they improve upon their social status. A few persons may become political leaders, Ministers, Cabinet Ministers or Chief Minister of a State. Many such examples can be found in the present day Indian polity. This has resulted into upward social mobility for them. Similarly, with greater political awareness with representatives in State assembly and Parliament they can (once the government to enact certain laws helping the lower segments of the society.

10) Modernization:

The process of modernization involves use of scientific knowledge and modern technology. It also refers to rationality and secular way of life. With the improvement in technology, people engaged in occupations of low prestige like scavengers discard their traditional occupations and take up occupations which are not dirty and have no polluting effects. In this way, they change their position upward. Similarly, the level of development of a country also facilitates or hinders social mobility. The less developed and traditional societies continue with old system of stratification and with accretive statuses. Whereas the developed and modern societies paved the way for greater opportunities and competition, it is only in the developed countries that there is a greater possibility of achieved statuses. In other words, modernization facilitates social mobility. Aspirations for moving upward also results in frustration and different mental and psychological problems. An individual is given to understand that he can achieve any status. But in reality this does not happens, his social background, birth in a race, ethnicity, facilitate or hinder his chances of social mobility. Similarly, the nations which do not have avenues for social mobility also suffer from stagnation and lack of development. In short, social mobility has both positive and negative consequences.

****

Review Questions

Q.1 Answers in 100 Words:

1) Explain the Concept of Social Stratification.
2) State the Characteristics of Social Stratification.
3) Explain the Functional Perspective of Social Stratification.
4) State the Concept of Social Mobility.
5) Explain the Concept of Vertical Mobility.

Q.2 Answers in 200 Words:

1) Explain the Perspectives of Social Stratification.
2) State the Factors affecting the Social Mobility.

Q.3 Answers in 300 Words:

1) What is Social Stratification? Explain the Forms of Social Stratification.
2) What is Social Mobility? State the Forms of Social Mobility.

Q.4 Write Short Note on Following:

1) Caste and Social Stratification.
2) Class and Social Stratification.
3) Gender and Social Stratification.
4) Power and Social Stratification.

****

UNIT 3

Communication & Mass Media

3.1 Social Change

3.2 Mass Media

Introduction:

People long for stability, security through continuity. However, no society remains static or stable. Society is constantly changing in its structure and function. This change in the society is inevitable. It's a continuous process. Some changes are willingly accepted by the society, some are not. Speed of change also varies from society to society. Some societies experience speedy change, some take long period. Social scientists are trying to understand the process of social change, the direction of social change and various factors that bring this social change. The word change refers to anything that is done differently. It does not necessarily mean the social change, because all the changes cannot be regarded as social changes.

Mass media is an integral part of society. It is crucial in information transfer and communication, as it covers a large audience. There are six main types of mass media, including digital, audience, electronic, print and traditional media. Television, newspapers, radio, and social media are typical examples of mass media. Mass media influences consumer behavior. For instance, most people believe that a good body is slim and curvy for women; while muscular for men due to the portrayal in social media. Mass media can have a negative effect, as it pushes people to violence and crime. Violent video games and films shown on social media and other platforms may influence teenage behavior, influencing them to imitate what they see with catastrophic consequences to the community and people involved. There is a need to increase control measures to mitigate the effects of media consumption on individuals.

3.1 Social Change:

According Fictor "Change means variations from previous state or mode of existence". Change is a universal phenomena i.e. it is a law of native. There's always a change in nature. Society is a part of nature and so society also changes and static society is unthinkable. Society is on the wheel of change, which may occur due to various factors (like demography, ideas etc. If there is any change in Technology etc. there's change in society) out the change varies in speed and farm. In some places the change is rapid whereas in other places it may be slow. These days due to industrialization and urbanization the change is rapid as compared to earlier times. The form may be economic, political, social (in striation) religious (in striation); change in any part of society affects all the other parts of society. E.g. an individual is the fundamental unit of society and there's change in the life of the individual which is called evolutionary process of social change (birth to death). This is a slow process.

3.1.1 Meaning:

Change means differentiation in anything observation over sometime. If we feel that there's come alteration we call it changes. It this change is in contest to social structure, institution etc., i.e. social context then it is social change. Social change may refer to the notion of social progress or sociocultural evolution, the philosophical idea that society moves forward by dialectical or evolutionary means. It may refer to a paradigmatic change in the socio-economic structure, for instance a shift away from feudalism and towards capitalism. Accordingly, it may also refer to social revolution, such as the Socialist revolution presented in Marxism, or to other social movements, such as Women's suffrage or the Civil rights movement. Social change may be driven by cultural, religious, economic, scientific or technological forces. Developmental psychology can play a role in social change. Social change comes about with tangible/intangible resource inputs as social investment.

3.1.2 Definitions:

Definitions of the social changes are as follows:

1) **T. B. Bottmore :**
   "Social change refers to change occurring in social structure or in institution or in the relationship between the institutions."
2) **According :**
   "Social change is change which occurs in the social organization i.e. its structure and function."
3) **Ginsberg:**
   "By social change is meant only such alternations as occur in social organization i.e. the structure and functions of society".
4) **Merril and Elbridge:**
   "Social change means, that large no. of persons are engaging in activities that differ from those which they or their immediate fore-fathers engaged in some time before."

5) Gillin and Gillin:

"Social changes are variations from the accepted mode of life, whether due to alteration in geographical condition, in cultural equipment, composition of the population. Or ideologies and whether brought about by diffusion or inventions within the group."

6) Jones:

"Social change is a term used to describe variations in or modification of any aspect of social process, social patterns, social interaction or social organization."

3.1.3 Factors of Social Change:

Factors of social change are as follows:

1) Physical Environment / Geographical Factor:

Certain geographic changes sometimes produce great social change. Climate, storms, social erosion, earthquakes, floods, droughts etc., definitely affect social life and induce social change. Human life is closely bound up with the geographical conditions of the earth. Human history is full of examples that flourishing civilisations fell prey to natural calamities. The distribution of population over various regions, the variations in the population densities, the agricultural production, flora and fauna, the joys and hardships all indicate a change when a change in the physical environment occurs. What to talk of rise and fall of civilisations, even our day-to-day life our clothes, eating material and habits, shelter design etc., all are influenced by the geographical conditions. Generally, changes in physical environment force migration of people in large numbers and this brings major changes in social life and cultural values also. Migration itself encourages change, for it brings a group into a new environment, subject to its new social contacts, and confronts it with new problems.

Though physical environment is an important factor which deeply affects social life, still it cannot be regarded as the only factor responsible for the growth of human society. This extreme approach was laid down by some geographical determinists, who held that geographical setting ultimately governs the form of society (family, marriage, economy, religion, government) and explains social change. But this is not true today. Now man is in the position to affect change in his physical environment. Men adapt themselves to their environment but they have the capacity to transform their physical environment according to their needs and requirements. Bennett and Tumin aptly remarked: "It is perhaps as reasonable, if not more so to insist that man modifies his physical environment rather than the environment modifies man."

2) Demographic (biological) Factor:

Broadly speaking, demography is concerned with the size and structure of human population. The social structure of a society is closely related with the changes in the size, composition and distri-bution of population. The size of the population is based mainly upon three factors birth rate, death rate and migration (immigration and emigration). The composition of population depends upon variables like age, sex, marital status, literacy etc. Changes in demographic structure, which may be caused by changes in mortality rates, will produce changes in the ratio of breadwinners to dependents.

Such a change can have consequences for the structure of family, kinship, political and other institutions. The size of population affects each of us quite personally. Whether we are born into a growing or a shrinking population has a bearing on our education, the age at which we marry our ability to get a job, the taxes we pay and many other factors. Population analysis shows that there is a relationship between population changes and economic, social and cultural variables like poverty, illiteracy, ill-health, family structure, forms of marriage, work etc. Population growth is the most important factor in poverty. Poverty is related with health and the size of the family also. Nations with large population (e.g., China and India) are more poverty- stricken than the countries which have not much population. Sex imbalance affects the forms of marriage (monogamy or polygyny). It is seen that communities, which have more males than females, resorted to polyandry system. Polygyny was generally found in such communities where females were in more numbers than males. The population of every society is always changing both in numbers as well as in composition. Population changes have occurred all through human history because of migration, war, pesti-lence, changing mores etc. In modern times, adoption of two artificial ways to population growth, viz., birth control and abortion are also affecting the number and composition of population structure. The decline of both the birth rate and the death rate bring social transfor-mation. With changes in size go changes in composition. While the birth rate is falling, the proportion of younger people in the proportion of youth's declines and that elders advances significant social changes occurs.

3) Cultural Factor:

It is an established fact that there is an intimate connection between our beliefs and social institutions, our values and social relationships. Values, beliefs, ideas, institutions are the basic elements of a culture. Certainly, all cultural changes involve social change. Social and the cultural aspects are closely interwoven. Thus, any change in the culture (ideas, values, beliefs etc.) brings a corresponding change in the whole social order. Social institutions cannot live on life shells within which life is extinct. Social systems are directly or indirectly the creations of cultural values. The history of culture offers many evidences which confirm the role of culture. A religious doctrine, which persisted with variations throughout many centuries, has affected the course of society. For instance, a certain attitude toward sex formulated by the Church Fathers in the early Middle Ages still hold good in the Catholic sect. Culture gives speed and direction to social change and deter-mines the limit beyond which social change cannot occur". If we choose to travel by a ship, the direction in which we travel is not predestinated by the design of the ship but it is the culture that decides the direction and the destination both. The port we sail to remains a cultural choice. Cultural factor is not only responsive to technological change but also acts back on it so as to influence its direction and its character. Cultural change in society has two major aspects:

a) Cultural change by discovery and invention, and

b) Cultural change by diffusion and borrowing.

The first comes from within a society and culture, and the second from another culture outside of the society. A discovery or an invention adds to the fund of our verified knowledge which later on becomes a factor of social change. Knowledge of bacterial infection brought about many changes in the behaviour of people in the form of prevention and cure of disease. Socio-cultural changes are also brought about by people from other cultures all over the world. Diffusion is the spread of cultural traits or patterns from group to group. Borrowing refers to the adoption of a cultural trait by people whose culture did not have that cultural trait. We have borrowed many cultural traits (such as use of knife and fork in eating) from Western culture.

Culture operates not only directly as a source of change but also indirectly, by its impact on the utilitarian order. This idea was best exemplified by a German sociologist Max Weber in his study of sociology of religion. In his study 'The Protestant Ethic and the Spirit of Capitalism', he saw that there is a direct relationship between the practical ethics of a religion and the character of its economic system, but he refused to accept the position that the letter determines the former as argued by Karl Marx. (Marx believed that the nature of a society is determined by the manner in which economy is owned and organised.) Though Weber too appreciated the importance of economic factors, but he did not ascribe to them the importance that they have in Marxian theory. For Marx economic influences were paramount and determined ell the rest, including religion, whereas for Weber economic phenomena themselves rest upon a broad ideological base and particularly upon religion. In his above mentioned study, Weber asserted that the devel-opment of modern capitalism could be attributed to Protestant reformation, particularly Calvinism. Protestantism emphasised the autonomy and independence of the individual rather than dependence on the church, priesthood and ritual. Weber argued that Calvinist Protestantism motivated men to seek worldly success. It laid emphasis on rational calculation, the willingness to accumulate for long-term profit and success and the emphasis on entrepreneurial success as a virtue. Weber maintained that the ideas, ideals and attitudes towards work (work is virtue, time lost, money lost etc.,), savings and life played an important role in the economic devel-opment of Western Europe and USA Protestanism provided much of the cultural content of early capitalism individualism, achievement motivation, hostility to inherited wealth and luxury, legitimation of entrepreneurial vocations, opposition to tradition and superstition, a commitment to organisation and calculation in personal and public life. In brief, Protestanism provided an element in the rationalisation (an important requirement of capitalism) of Western society. Weber did not simply explained capitalist development in terms of religious belief, but argued that the religious factor, if combined with others, of a political, economic and social nature, can produce a certain type of social change.

4) Ideational Factor:

Among the cultural factors affecting social change in modern times, the development of science and secularisation of thought have contributed a lot to the development of the critical and innovative character of the modern outlook. We no longer follow many customs or habits merely because they have the age-old authority of tradition. On the contrary, our ways of life have increasingly become on the basis of rationality. Some writers have interpreted social change at ideational level and asserted that all social change is ideational. They argued that ideas could influence the course of social change. For them, ideational changes are important contributory factors to many or most types of social change. Ideas and ideologies together are powerful motivating forces in social change. For instance, after independence, the directive principles equality, fraternity, liberty and justice laid down in our constitution have not only revolutionised the Indian society but it has even affected greatly the relations between the members of the family. Social philosophers, who believed in the force of ideas, argued that no material or social factors can produce change unless there is also a change in ideas within society or ideas about society and nature. In modern times, not only the way we think, but the contents of ideas have also changed. Ideals of self-betterment, freedom, equality and democratic participation are largely creations of the past two/ three centuries. Such ideals have served to mobilise processes of social and political change, including reformation movements and revolutions.

5) Economic Factor:

Of economic influences, the most far-reaching is the impact of indus-trialisation. It has revolutionised the whole way of life, institutions, organisations and community life. In traditional production systems, levels of production were fairly static since they were geared to habitual, customary needs. Modern industrial capitalism promotes the constant revision of the technology of production, a process into which science is increasingly drawn. The impact of industrialisation (science and technology) we can easily see on Indian family system (joint family) and caste system. (For detailed analysis of the influence of economic factor, see Marx's views discussed in Economic Theory of Social Change).

6) Political Factor:

State is the most powerful organisation which regulates the social relationships. It has the power to legislate new laws, repeal old ones to bring social change in the society. Laws regarding child marriage, widow remarriage, divorce, inheritance and succession, untouchability are some of the examples which have brought many changes in the social structure of Indian society. The type of political leadership and individuals in power also influences the rate and direction of social change. In many societies the political leadership controls the economy also. Scientific-technological and non-techno-logical change are also dependent on political development which indirectly affects social change. There is a direct relationship between the type of political organisation and social change. In hunting and gathering societies, there were no political organisation capable of mobilising the community, as such; there were minimum changes in the societies. In all other types of society, however, the existence of distinct political agencies, such as chiefs, lords, kings and governments strongly affects the course of development of society takes. A ruler may choose to channel resources into building up his castle, for example, even when this impoverishes most of the population. Political development in the last two or three centuries (in India especially after independence) has certainly influenced economic change as much as economic change has influenced politics. Govern-ments now play a major role in stimulating (and sometimes retarding) rates of economic growth. In all industrial societies there is high level of state intervention in production.

7) Technological Factors:

The technological factors also play important role in causing social change. Then what is technology? How it brings social change? In the study of sociology, technology has a wider connotation. It implies an appropriate organization and systematic application of scientific knowledge to meet the human requirements. Technology is a product of utilization. When the scientific knowledge is applied to the problems of life, it becomes technology. Technology is fast growing. Modern age is the "Age of Technology".

According to W. F. Ogburn, "Technology changes society by changing our environments to which we In turn adopt. This change is usually in the material environment and the adjustment that we make with these changes often modifies customs and social institution initiates a corresponding social change.

Sources of Technological Change:

There are mainly two important sources of technological change. They are:

i) Inventions:

Invention denotes creation of new ways of using existing knowledge or new ways of combining existing artifacts. A single invention in technology can produce a large scale change in society. One important example of invention is the invention of automobile.

ii) Discovery:

Discovery means the new way of looking at the environment. Technological innovation originates also from another source called discovery. Example-Discovery of modern medicines is the result of discoveries in biology and partly the result of invention. Invention and discovery are significant characteristic of our age. Apart from these two, there are three technological factors which are mainly responsible for social change.

3.2 Mass Media:

Mass media refers to a diverse array of media that reach a large audience via mass communication. Broadcast media transmit information electronically via media such as films, radio, recorded music, or television. Digital media comprises both Internet and mobile mass communication. Internet media comprise such services as email, social media sites, websites, and Internet-based radio and television. Many other mass media outlets have an additional presence on the web, by such means as linking to or running TV ads online, or distributing QR codes in outdoor or print media to direct mobile users to a website. In this way, they can use the easy accessibility and outreach capabilities the Internet affords, as thereby easily broadcast information throughout many different regions of the world simultaneously and cost-efficiently. Outdoor media transmit information via such media as AR advertising; billboards; blimps; flying billboards (signs in tow of airplanes); placards or kiosks placed inside and outside buses, commercial buildings, shops, sports stadiums, subway cars, or trains; signs; or skywriting. Print media transmit information via physical objects, such as books, comics, magazines, newspapers, or pamphlets. Event organising and public speaking can also be considered forms of mass media.

3.2.1 Meaning:

To put it simply, Mass Media can be defined as a technology which is intended to communicate or reach a mass audience. Mass media is the primary means of communication for the general public to communicate with each other as well as on a grander level. The most popular types of mass media include Newspapers, Radio, Television, Internet, Magazines and more.

3.2.2 Print Media:

Print Media is also known as press advertising. It is one of the media of communication along with broadcast media and outdoor advertising media. It mainly includes advertising through newspaper and magazines. The components of print-media i.e. newspapers and magazines are also known as media-vehicles. Media vehicle carries advertisers message to the target audience Print media is a traditional method of reaching the target audience. It is the oldest and most popular media. Print media is mainly of two types.

A) Meaning:

The word print originates from the Middle English word 'print' which means to 'to impress or stamps'. It is a process of producing text using ink, lettering and paper or other printable materials. The origin of media goes back to the Latin word Medias or medium. This means an intermediate agency or channel of communication. Print media is also as press media. Print media plays an important part in educating, informing, entertaining and influencing the lives of people worldwide. This form of media stimulates the eyes through visual images and also the intellect through the text and information available to readers.

B) Types of Print Media:

Following are the types of print media:

1) Newspapers Media:

Newspapers are bought largely for their news values. Newspaper may be national, local, weekly, daily. Newspapers are published in various languages. In India, maximum newspapers are published in Hindi and English. A good number of newspapers are also published in different regional languages. Different newspapers differ in their circulation. The word circulation refers to number of copies sold in a particular period of time.

2) Magazines and Journals:

Magazines and journals are another form of print-media. These are published periodically at regular intervals like fortnightly, monthly, quarterly, and annually. Magazines serve the educational, informational and entertainment needs of readers.

3) Booklets and Brochures:

Booklets and brochures are a part of promotional literature of product. There are two types of booklets and brochures.

i) Pre-buying Promotion:

Usually in malls and stores, promotional literature is distributed free to all (with discount offers, or other schemes which seems profitable). For example a free booklet about cosmetics will include information about the products, latest trends, contents, the benefits of using them, the available range, or color, discount coupons, which will most likely which have a positive impact on decision-making of the prospective customer.

ii) Post buying Promotion:

These booklets and brochures are usually given with a product for better customer experience and easy usages, post purchasing. It is to be observed that a product is usually accompanied with a small booklet giving detail about the benefit of using the product, usage direction, cleaning and storage instructions. The guidelines are usually followed by series of „how to images" which facilitate to easy information about the product. These booklets may also include „other offering" section. Organization also has their own profiles in the form of brochures which they give to their stakeholder to create a favorable image. It highlights the information about the company, its capacity and capability, service and solution offered milestone achievements, sustainability, innovation, award, etc.

4) House Magazine, Periodical or Newsletter:

Most of the organizations today have learned that it is important to communicate with all the stockholders in order to be successful. Hence, the customer, shareholder, investors, solicitors and employees are updated about the activities of the organization from time to time. Many organizations today invent various platforms like house magazines, periodicals, or newsletters to keep the stockholders posted about the news related to the company.

5) Books:

It is a collection of sheets of paper, parchment or other material with a piece of text written on them, bound together along one edge within covers. A book is also literary work or main division of such a work. A book may be in hard copy or in electronic format. A book produced in electronic format is called or known as „e-book". Books are significant medium of mass communication as they have larger reader base. The expressions and opinions of the writer are taken to the readers in the form of a compiled book.

C) Advantages of Print Media:

Following are the advantages of print media:

1) Appeal to Visual Learners:

Flashy images in magazines get the attention of many magazine readers. Thus if you have a killer ad design, the results are always promising.

2) Still gives a Higher ROI than Digital Ads:

There is a high tendency for print media to keep at homes and re-read and shared. Newspapers and magazines at the doctor's office, the library or public places, have a long shelf life which increases your ad's exposure. Following gives print ads higher chances to stick than digital ads which forget instantly.

3) Loyal Customer base:

Print media has a large loyal customer base that buys the publication on a weekly or monthly basis for months, maybe even for years. Thus you are assured of massive exposure for your advertisement with print media.

4) Flexible:

Print media advertising comes with many options. From features, full-page ads to small ad listings it gives you the flexibility in selecting the type of ad to fit your requirements and budget.

5) **Establish Trust:**
Researches show that prints media is one of the most trusted media outlets out there. Since people purchase from those who they trust, advertising on print media can attract you more sales than any other media outlets.

6) **Reach Multiple Generations:**
Consumers of newspapers and magazines can range from teens, young adults to senior citizens, enabling you to target a wide range of audience easily.

7) **Best for Local Targeting:**
If you are a local business or an organization, it's the best way to spread your message or promote your business. You can easily hand out leaflets in public areas and get your ads to publish on local newspapers to spread awareness among the local community.

D) **Disadvantages of Print Media:**
Following are the disadvantages of print media:

1) **Not for a Global Audience:**
Print media is not the best method to get the word out about your business if you are targeting a global audience as it's very rare to find print publications that read globally.

2) **Requires a lot of Planning:**
Getting published on print media is quite a process. You will have to plan your ad, write an ad copy, hire someone to design it for you and submit the ad copy to the publication and process the payment. The process can be time-consuming and complex.

3) **Hard to Target a Specific Audience:**
With print media, it's hard to target specific audiences. For example, targeting people who want to buy a camera is not possible with print media like weekly newspapers.

4) **Might not stand out:**
There's always a chance that your ad to get disappear among other ads as print media publish a lot of advisement per edition even if you pay for a full-page advertisement.

5) **Higher Cost:**
Getting published on print media can be highly expensive.

3.2.3 Electronic Media:

It includes advertisement in radio, television, cable etc. This media has both audio and visual effect. Broadcast is a media carrying advertiser's message to the target-audience. Radios, Television are media vehicles of broadcast advertising. TV has grown faster than any other advertising media and offers combination of sight, sound and movement in presenting advertisements. TV and radio are most persuasive media. With the growth of cable network, various satellite-channels have become available. It has promoted competition among TV channels which has reduced their ad-charges. It has made possible for the medium-scale-advertisers to use TV for their advertising campaign. Moreover, advertisement in Cable TV is within the reach of even smaller advertisers. Broadcast media is mainly of two types: (a) Television (b) Radio.

A) Meaning:

Electronic media is anything that is used to advertise or promote a thing, Person, Product etc., electronically. This is quite a wide subject and there are many different things that fall into this category. There are more and more channels for electronic media that come out as our technology grows and expands. Electronic media are media that use electronics or electromechanical energy for the end-user (audience) to access the content. This is in contrast to static media (mainly print media), which today are most often created electronically, but don't require electronics to be accessed by the end-user in the printed form. The primary electronic media sources familiar to the general public are better known as video recordings, audio recordings, multimedia presentations, slide presentations, CD-ROM and online content. Most new media are in the form of digital media. However, an electronic media may be in either analog or digital format.

B) Types of Electronic Media:

Following are the types of electronic media:

1) Television Media:

Commercial television advertising was introduced in India in 1976. With the reduction In TV prices and increase in economic status of an average Indian, availability of TV sets has increased tremendously. TV makes full use of sight, sound and motion and has maximum impact on audience. The coverage of television is increasing at a rapid pace in India. Television advertising is in the form of sponsorship and participation. Sponsorship means sponsoring a particular programme by advertiser. In this case, advertiser makes payment to TV channel for sponsoring a programme. The sponsor is allowed generally 15% of total time of TV programme to show his advertisement or to sell this time to other advertisers. Sometimes two or more advertisers co-sponsor a TV programme. In case of participation, advertiser pays to TV channel for 10.15, 20, 30 seconds of commercial time during prescribed TV programme i.e. advertiser makes direct payment to TV channel for telecasting his advertisement. So in case of sponsorship, advertiser sponsors the TV programme, while in case of participation, advertises does-not sponsor T.V programme, but makes payment to TV channel for telecasting its advertisement. Rates of advertisement differ from one channel to other channel. Even in case of same channel, these rates differ from one programme to other programme.

2) Radio Media:

The advertising message is convey through spoken words in case of radio-advertising. Over the years radio had remained popular and effective means of advertising. With the growth in TV, radios popularity has come down. But there was a time, when almost every person of India used to listen radio programmes. Radio commercials were started in India in the year 1967. This mode is still popular among illiterates, poor segment and in rural areas. In India FM broadcasting was opened for private sector on 15 August 1993. After the privatisation of this channel, its quality has improved FM stands for "Frequency Modulation" FM channel sound has stereo phonic quality and is free from disturbance due to weather changes; because of this feature, FM. broadcasting has become popular. With the introduction of FM broadcasting radio listener ship has increased once again in rural areas as well as in urban areas.

3) Internet:

Advertising on the internet has become increasingly popular as you can advertise to your target audience. Space can be bought on websites that the target customers would use and data can be collected about how many people clicked on the ad. This, in turn, gives the company figures and statistics about how successful the advertising has been.

4) Electronic Advertising:

Advertising on screens at bus stops, shopping centres and on ATM screens have also increased in the last decade. These usually advertise amenities and shops that are close by so that consumers will have them fresh in their minds when they are in the area.

5) Outdoor Advertising Media:

Advertising media is a vehicle or device that carries the message of the advertiser to the target consumer. Through an advertisement, information or message regarding the advertising product or the advertiser is passed on to the consumers or persons concerned. These are a number of media available to the advertiser for advertising the goods and services and he has to select right types of medium. One such media is outdoor advertising. Historically, it is the oldest form of advertising and remains the most common medium even today. Outdoor advertising is meant for the moving public and provides the advantages of reminding the people frequently of the products and their specialities. It is also known as position, mural or indirect advertising. Outdoor advertising is literally out of door, i.e., it is out of the home or place of business. Outdoor advertising media is made up of vehicles like, posters painted displays, hoardings, and electronic signs, travelling displays, skywriting and the like.

6) Films:

Films are considered a major mass medium because of their mass appeal and influence on society. „Film" is a term that encompasses motion pictures or individual projects, as well as the field in general. The origin of term "films" came from "photographic film" (also called film stock). It was historically the primary medium for recording and displaying motion picture. Films are produced by recording the movements of people and objects with "camera" or creating them using „animation" technique and "special effects". They comprise a series of individual frames. When these images are shown rapidly in succession, the illusion of motion is given to viewer. Flickering between frames is not seen due to an effect known as persistence of vision whereby the eyes retain a visual image for a fraction of second after the sources has been removed. Films are considered by many to be an important art form.

7) New Age Media:

With the advent of internet, we are now enjoying the benefit of high technology mass media, which is not only faster than the old school mass media, but also has a widespread range. Mobile phones, computers, and internet are often referred to as the new-age media. Internet has opened up several new opportunities for mass communication which includes email, websites, e-forums, e-books, blogging, internet TV and many others which are booming today. Sites like Facebook, Twitter and YouTube had made communication to the masses all the more entertaining, interesting and easier.

8) Mobile Phones:

Mobile phone were introduced in Japan in 1979 but became a mass media only in 1998 when the first downloadable ringing tones were introduced in Finland. Soon most form of media content were introduced one mobile phone, and today total values of media consumed on mobile towers over that of internet content. The mobile media content includes mobile music which includes ringing tone, ring back tones, true tones, MP3files, Karaoke, music video, music streaming services, etc. mobile gaming and various news, entertainment and advertising services. In Japan mobile phone are very popular. Similar to the internet, mobiles are also interactive media, like email on the internet. The top application on mobile is also personal massaging service, but text massaging is used by many people. Practically all internet services and applications exists have similar cousins on mobile, from search to multiplayer games to virtual worlds to blogs. Mobile has several unique benefits which many mobile media pundits claim that mobile is a more powerful carried and always connected communication device. Mobile has the best audience accuracy and is the only mass media with a build in payment channel available to every user without any credit cards or payable

9) Computer:

With the invention of computer the impossible has become possible. We virtually get information about everything from pin to piano with the help of computer. It has added speed and multimedia to the information which was earlier available only in the print format. Anyone can voice their opinions through computers. Computers have added a new breakthrough in the mass media by cutting edge technology.

10) Internet:

This is most important devoice of the new age media. The discovery of internet can be called the biggest invention in mass media. In earlier days, news used to reach people only with the morning newspaper, but today, live updates reach us simultaneously as the events unfold. For example, the royal wedding of Kate Middleton and Prince William was watched live on the internet by millions of people around the world. Internet has inspired interaction and connectivity through its social networking medium. It has become one of the core means of mass communication. One cannot think of leading the life without it.

C) Advantages of Electronic Media:

Following are the advantages of electronic media:

1) Speedy Transmission:

It requires only a few seconds to communicate through electronic media because it supports quick transmission.

2) Wide Coverage:

World has become a global village and communication around the globe requires a second only.

3) Low Cost:

Electronic communication saves time and money. For example, Text SMS is cheaper than the traditional letter.

4) Exchange of Feedback:

Electronic communication allows the instant exchange of feedback. So communication becomes perfect using electronic media.

5) Managing Global Operation:

Due to the advancement of electronic media, business managers can easily control operation across the globe. Video or teleconferencing e-mail and mobile communication are helping managers in this regard.

D) Disadvantages of Electronic Media:

Following are the disadvantages of electronic media:

1) The Volume of Data:

The volume of telecommunication information is increasing at such a fast rate that business people are unable to absorb it within the relevant time limit.

2) The Cost of Development:

Electronic communication requires huge investment for infrastructural development. Frequent change in technology also demands further investment.

3) Legal Status:

Data or information, if faxed, may be distorted and will cause zero value in the eye of law.

4) Undelivered Data:

Data may not be retrieved due to system error or fault with the technology. Hence required service will be delayed

5) Dependency:

Technology is changing every day and therefore poor countries face the problem as they cannot afford the new or advanced technology. Therefore poor countries need to be dependent towards developed countries for sharing global network.

3.2.4 Social Media:

Social media is internet-based and gives users quick electronic communication of content. Content includes personal information, documents, videos, and photos. Users engage with social media via computer, tablet or Smartphone via web-based software or web application, often utilizing it for messaging.

A) Meaning of Social Media:

The Merriam-Webster Dictionary defines social media as: "Forms of electronic communication (such as websites for social networking and micro-blogging) through which users create online communities to share information, ideas, personal messages, and other content (such as videos)."

The Cambridge Dictionary defines social media as "Websites and computer programs that allow people to communicate and share information on the internet using a computer or mobile phone."

The Oxford Dictionary definition is more or less the same. According to it, social media can be defined as "Websites and applications that enable users to create and share content or to participate in social networking."

B) Features of Social Media:

Following are the features of social media:

1) Provide Free Web Space:

Members of these sites don't need to own or share web servers. They can publish their content on the free space provided by these sites.

2) Provide Free Web Address:

Members are allotted a unique web address that becomes the web identity of an individual or a business. It can be used to identify, connect and share content.

3) **Ask Members to build Profiles:**

These sites require members to build their profiles. Information entered in the profiles is used to connect friends and contacts, and build networks that connect people with similar likes and interests across the world.

4) **Encourage Members to upload Content:**

These sites allow members to upload text messages, photographs, audio and video files. All posts are published in descending order with the last post coming first. Most important, all content is published in real time, and can be read, viewed or shared instantly.

5) **Allow Members to build Conversations:**

Members can browse content and comment upon it. By doing so, social media sites allow members to engage in conversations that increase engagement.

6) **Allow Live Chats:**

Several social media sites have chat clients that enable members to chat with each other in real time.

7) **Direct Messaging Facility:**

Several social media sites provide direct messaging facility to their members. This allows members to send private messages, which can be read or viewed only by those for whom the message is intended.

8) **Provide Tagging Alerts:**

Most social media sites alert members through e-mail or in site notifications whenever they are tagged in a message or in a photograph.

C) Components of Social Media:

Following are the components of social media:

1) **Email:**

Email or electronic mails have drastically reduced the time it took for drafting and sending letters, or mails. Electronic mails have also facilitated lesser usage of paper.

2) **Websites:**

Internet has a plethora of websites dedicated to various people, companies, activities, etc. The most significant utility of these websites is providing information through search engines, downloads through libraries, and interaction through the social networking sites. Because of these websites, carrying out e-commerce transactions has also become easy.

3) **Podcasts:**

Podcasts are medium of mass communication that includes short video or audio files. They can be seen and heard on mobiles, computers and portable media instruments. They are engaging devices of communication.

4) E-Forums:

E-forums are bulletin boards on websites where people start threads on topics. These are usually hosted on a websites. These forums are open platform to discuss a range of topics from which wall color is appropriate for baby girl's room to the research on the God particle. People give their opinions and share their experiences on various topics.

5) E-books:

There are number of websites which has hosted eBooks and online libraries. The main benefit of having eBooks is that one need not carry bulky books. They can be read on eBook readers, mobiles computer screens or other devices. The font size can be adjusted to requirements

6) Blogging:

A blog is a space on the internet where a single person or group of people records their information, opinion, photos, videos, etc. It is an interesting and free platform to talk about any topic. Interaction happens in the form of comments on feedback.

7) Internet TV:

It is also known as online TV. It usually has an archive of programs. You have to choose the program you wish to view from the list. The programs can be viewed directly from the host server, or download the content on computer. It is an effective means of communication.

8) Facebook:

It is the most popular social networking website. Facebook has several applications which people utilize. It is the best platform to meet old friends, or make new ones. Advertisers also like this forum for communicating about their products.

9) Twitter:

It is also famous networking website. Twitter is micro blogging site which allows interaction and feedback of different people. There was time when it was very popular among celebrities and individuals. Today, the governments of various nations have understood the importance of "tweeting" information to the public, and regularly share information through Twitter.

10) You Tube:

It is a websites which uploads content in a video format. It houses a large range of interesting videos that appeal to people of all generations. From films to educational videos, everything could be found on YouTube.

11) Wikipedia:

It is an absolved web book, customized to give a layman insight about glorious to most undignified things prevailing in the world. From living to non-living beings, it accustoms online reference book made through the community oriented exertion of a group of clients known as Wikipedia's. Anybody enrolled on the site can write an article for distribution; enlistment is not needed to alter articles. The webpage's name originates from wiki, a server program that empowers anybody to alter website content through their web program.

12) LinkedIn:

LinkedIn is a social system administration site planned particularly for the business group. The objective of the site is to permit enrolled parts to secure and archive systems of individuals they know and trust professionally.

3.2.5 Impact of Mass Media on Society:

Mass media is communication whether written, broadcast, or spoken that reaches a large audience. This includes television, radio, advertising, movies, the Internet, newspapers, magazines, and so forth.

Mass media is a significant force in modern culture, particularly in America. Sociologists refer to this as a mediated culture where media reflects and creates the culture. Communities and individuals are bombarded constantly with messages from a multitude of sources including TV, billboards, and magazines, to name a few. These messages promote not only products, but moods, attitudes, and a sense of what is and is not important. Mass media makes possible the concept of celebrity: without the ability of movies, magazines, and news media to reach across thousands of miles, people could not become famous. In fact, only political and business leaders, as well as the few notorious outlaws, were famous in the past. Only in recent times have actors, singers, and other social elites become celebrities or "stars."

The current level of media saturation has not always existed. As recently as the 1960s and 1970s, television, for example, consisted of primarily three networks, public broadcasting, and a few local independent stations. These channels aimed their programming primarily at two-parent, middle-class families. Even so, some middle-class households did not even own a television. Today, one can find a television in the poorest of homes, and multiple TVs in most middle-class homes. Not only has availability increased, but programming is increasingly diverse with shows aimed to please all ages, incomes, backgrounds, and attitudes. This widespread availability and exposure makes television the primary focus of most mass-media discussions. More recently, the Internet has increased its role exponentially as more businesses and households "sign on." Although TV and the Internet have dominated the mass media, movies and magazines—particularly those lining the aisles at grocery checkout stands—also play a powerful role in culture, as do other forms of media.

What role does mass media play? Legislatures, media executives, local school officials, and sociologists have all debated this controversial question. While opinions vary as to the extent and type of influence the mass media wields, all sides agree that mass media is a permanent part of modern culture. Three main sociological perspectives on the role of media exist: the limited-effects theory, the class-dominant theory, and the culturalist theory.

1) Limited-effects Theory:

The limited-effects theory argues that because people generally choose what to watch or read based on what they already believe, media exerts a negligible influence. This theory originated and was tested in the 1940s and 1950s. Studies that examined the ability of media to influence voting found that well-informed people relied more on personal experience, prior knowledge, and their own reasoning. However, media "experts" more likely swayed those who were less informed. Critics point to two problems with this perspective. First, they claim that limited-effects theory ignores the media's role in framing and limiting the discussion and debate of issues. How media frames the debate and what questions members of the media ask change the outcome of the discussion and the possible conclusions people may draw. Second, this theory came into existence when the availability and dominance of media was far less widespread.

2) Class-dominant Theory:

The class-dominant theory argues that the media reflects and projects the view of minority elite, which controls it. Those people who own and control the corporations that produce media comprise these elite. Advocates of this view concern themselves particularly with massive corporate mergers of media organizations, which limit competition and put big business at the reins of media especially news media. Their concern is that when ownership is restricted, a few people then have the ability to manipulate what people can see or hear. For example, owners can easily avoid or silence stories that expose unethical corporate behavior or hold corporations responsible for their actions.

The issue of sponsorship adds to this problem. Advertising dollars fund most media. Networks aim programming at the largest possible audience because the broader the appeal, the greater the potential purchasing audience and the easier selling air time to advertisers becomes. Thus, news organizations may shy away from negative stories about corporations (especially parent corporations) that finance large advertising campaigns in their newspaper or on their stations. Television networks receiving millions of dollars in advertising from companies like Nike and other textile manufacturers were slow to run stories on their news shows about possible human-rights violations by these companies in foreign countries. Media watchers identify the same problem at the local level where city newspapers will not give new cars poor reviews or run stories on selling a home without an agent because the majority of their funding comes from auto and real estate advertising. This influence also extends to programming. In the 1990s a network cancelled a short-run drama with clear religious sentiments, Christy, because, although highly popular and beloved in rural America, the program did not rate well among young city dwellers that advertisers were targeting in ads.

Critics of this theory counter these arguments by saying that local control of news media largely lies beyond the reach of large corporate offices elsewhere, and that the quality of news depends upon good journalists. They contend that those less powerful and not in control of media have often received full media coverage and subsequent support. As examples they name numerous environmental causes, the anti-nuclear movement, the anti-Vietnam movement, and the pro-Gulf War movement.

While most people argue that a corporate elite controls media, a variation on this approach argues that a politically "liberal" elite controls media. They point to the fact that journalists, being more highly educated than the general population, hold more liberal political views, consider themselves "left of center," and are more likely to register as Democrats. They further point to examples from the media itself and the statistical reality that the media more often labels conservative commentators or politicians as "conservative" than liberals as "liberal."

Media language can be revealing, too. Media uses the terms "arch" or "ultra" conservative, but rarely or never the terms "arch" or "ultra" liberal. Those who argue that a political elite controls media also point out that the movements that have gained media attention the environment, anti-nuclear, and anti-Vietnam generally support liberal political issues. Predominantly conservative political issues have yet to gain prominent media attention, or have been opposed by the media. Advocates of this view point to the Strategic Arms Initiative of the 1980s Reagan administration. Media quickly characterized the defense program as "Star Wars," linking it to an expensive fantasy. The public failed to support it, and the program did not get funding or congressional support.

3) Culturalist Theory:

The culturalist theory, developed in the 1980s and 1990s, combines the other two theories and claims that people interact with media to create their own meanings out of the images and messages they receive. This theory sees audiences as playing an active rather than passive role in relation to mass media. One strand of research focuses on the audiences and how they interact with media; the other strand of research focuses on those who produce the media, particularly the news.

Theorists emphasize that audiences choose what to watch among a wide range of options, choose how much to watch, and may choose the mute button or the VCR remote over the programming selected by the network or cable station. Studies of mass media done by sociologist's parallel text-reading and interpretation research completed by linguists (people who study language). Both groups of researchers find that when people approach material, whether written text or media images and messages, they interpret that material based on their own knowledge and experience. Thus, when researchers ask different groups to explain the meaning of a particular song or video, the groups produce widely divergent interpretations based on age, gender, race, ethnicity, and religious background. Therefore, culturalist theorists claim that, while a few elite in large corporations may exert significant control over what information media produces and distributes personal perspective plays a more powerful role in how the audience members interpret those messages.

★★★★★★★

Review Questions

Q.1 Answers in 100 Words:

1) Explain the Concept of Social Change.
2) State the Characteristics of Social Stratification.
3) Explain the Functional Perspective of Social Stratification.
4) State the Concept of Social Mobility.
5) Explain the Concept of Vertical Mobility.

Q.2 Answers in 200 Words:

1) Explain the advantages and disadvantages of Print Media.
2) State the Types of Electronic Media.
3) What is Social Media? Explain the Features of Social Media.
4) Explain the Components of Social Media.

Q.3 Answers in 300 Words:

1) What is Social Change? Explain the Factors of Social Change.
2) Discuss in detail about the Print Media.
3) What is Electronic Media? Explain the advantages and disadvantages of Electronic Media.
4) Discuss in detail the Impact of Mass Media on Society.

Q.4 Write Short Note on Following:

1) Social Change.
2) Mass Media.
3) Print Media.
4) Electronic Media.
5) Social Media.

★★★★★★★

UNIT

4

Application of Sociology

Introduction:

Sociology seeks to deepen our understanding of human relationships by unravelling new truths about them. It helps in removing ignorance about human relationships. It is relevant wherever human relations are at work. Whatever the field the emphasis will be on understanding human behaviour and relationships. 'Sociology enables us to understand the world we live in but also to understand ourselves, for we are the products of that world. This understanding can help us to gain more control over our lives but it can also be put to more practical uses as well'. In fact, it can be argued that sociology is indispensable for understanding the present complex world. There are several reasons why sociological knowledge is essential in making sense of the contemporary world. 'Sociology is not only an intellectual discipline, it is also a profession ... when we speak of a profession, we refer mainly to themes as the uses or applications of a body of knowledge'. The student may sometimes get confused about sociology and social reform. But sociology is not social reform. The essential principles of sociology are a prerequisite in any study of human relationships and in any proposed solution to a social problem. It is desirable, of course, that 'solutions' be found for the problems of society and that certain universal principles of social life be established. A student may study sociology for his own sake, just to know more about society and culture. But mere knowledge does not satisfy him. He may probably seek sociological knowledge just to apply it to the social situations in which he finds himself. In general, it may be said that sociological knowledge lends itself to helping an individual and his society achieve results in terms of better social relations. But, a very few students pursue the subject of sociology to either seek knowledge for knowledge sake or applying it in the solution of their own day-to-day life problems.

4.1 Applied Sociology:

Applied sociology uses information about society and social forces or actions to solve social issues. The goal of applied sociology is to use theories, concepts, and methods to solve real-world problems (Steele and Price 2008). This form of sociological practice is the application of sociology to improve society, not rebuild it or create social reform as with public sociology. Applied sociologists use sociology to address a specific social issue for a specific group of people. This form of practice applies sociological principles and methods to enhance human social life by using analyzing, evaluating, and suggesting interventions or solutions grounded in theory.

4.1.1 Meaning:

Applied sociology is using the sociological tools to "understand, intervene, or enhance human social life. People apply sociology when they use sociological methods, theories, concepts, or perspectives (tools) to address a social problem or issue. Lots of social scientists 'use' sociological tools in their teaching or in their research. But only a subset uses those tools to plan or engage in direct, concurrent social intervention or enhancement. We generally refer to those that do as applied sociologists. Many different approaches to sociological application exist. We use the term 'sociological practice' or 'practitioner' to inclusively refer to applied, clinical, and public sociologists, as well as those who identify more with methodology used across the social sciences: community-based researchers, participatory-action researchers, and translational researchers.

4.1.2 Meaning:

According to G.R. Madan, the main task of applied sociology is to deal with social problems. From the point of view of applied sociology, social problems are divided into two categories that are (i) problems of social disorganisation or social rehabilitation, and (ii) problems of social recon-struction. The first category includes problems of deviants, defectives and dependents, e.g. crimi-nals, delinquents, orphans, mentally defectives, ills, blinds, etc. For the problems of this kind, mea-sures are needed to cope with the evil. They are generally curative or rehabilitative in character.

1) **Clinical Sociology:**

   It refers to the use of sociological knowledge in providing assistance to individuals and organisations. This term, analogous to clinical psychology, was introduced in 1931 by Chicago sociologist Louis Wirth for the work of sociologists employed in clinical settings alongside social workers, psychologists, and psychiatrists. Clinical sociology involves the use of sociological knowledge to aid diagnosis, treatment, teaching and research. A clinical sociologist may study the ways of improving employee morale.

2) **Social Engineering:**

It attempts to use sociological knowledge to design social policies or institutions with a specific purpose. It refers to planned social change and social development. The planned improvement of society is practically impossible without the scientific knowledge provided by sociology. Social engineering involves the intelligent application of sociological knowledge. It is based on the idea that governments can shape and manage key features of society; in much the same way as the economy is managed. For example, the extent of women's employment is clearly determined in part by government policy to promote to impede women's paid work. For doing such works, applied sociologists use social indicators and social trend reports. Every family, school, club, business and local bodies recognises and pursues its goal. This is nothing more or less than social engineering.

3) **Social Work:**

Though it is a distinct discipline, it is considered as applied aspect of sociology. Social work is the field in which the principles of the social sciences, especially sociology, are applied to actual social problems in the same way the principles of physiology are applied in medicine or the principles of economics are applied in business management. A social worker might, for example, use information obtained from family research to try to place children in foster homes or to establish centres of spouse abuse. The term 'social work' is applied to the various organised methods for promoting human welfare through the prevention and relief of suffering. In the late nineteenth century, social work was largely voluntary (notably as a charitable activity). Since the Second World War, social work practice has become increasingly professionalised. In India, many institutions of social work training and education were established; notable among them is the renowned Tata Institute of Social Work, Mumbai. Many state governments have also started such institutions on its pattern. These institutions have the aim to train people to step out into society and to assist in the solution of its immediate problems.

4) **Applied Social Research:**

It is similar in many respects to the basic/pure research conducted in universities and colleges. At one end of the continuum of social research would be the disciplines involved in research, not to solve a specific problem, but simply to increase our understanding of the social world. Such researches are known as pure/basic research. At the other end of the continuum would be the disciplines that use knowledge to solve actual problems, these researches is called applied social research. Social workers devise their own research methods and techniques to help people solve personal and group problems, and the resulting applications contribute to our existing body of knowledge. Applied social research may take the form of descriptive research, survey research, analytical or evaluation research such as systematic attempts to estimate the potential effects of a proposed social programme or effects of planned change or a new approach to management in a business firms.

5) Action Sociology:

Action sociology is also a form of applied sociology in which sociologist is asked to participate in the development process and tackle vital social problems actively. It is directly concerned with the solutions of the social problems. It requires the involvement of the sociologist in all stages of development or the solutions of the problem. This means not only to find out the roots of the social problem and suggest it remedy but to associate ourselves in the diagnosis of the problem, planning, execution, monitoring and evaluation of the programme designed to solve the problem. In India, a fine example of this approach (action sociology) we find in the project of Sulabh International started by a sociologist Bindeshwar Pathak.

Action sociology/action research places emphasis on the sociologist not only to work as a researcher but to assume the role of a change agent also. Such change agents are often used in local communities, local bodies or in companies as consultants. They work as part of the change process itself. This view was supported by Herbert Gans. He wrote: "I believe that the sociologist ought to be more than a detached researcher and he should participate more directly in social action programmes. The sociologist can help to develop the means necessary to achieve the goals, i.e., by participating in the development of programmes of action. It is here that he can perhaps make his most useful contribution."

Currently, there is a strong trend toward action sociology. Indeed, radical sociologists maintain that radical sociology is sociology of engagement. Recently, French sociologist Alain Touraine developed a radical new theoretical framework known as actionalism. He claimed that the sociologist is an agent of change, not a neutral observer.

4.2 Career with Sociology:

Sociology is not only an intellectual discipline, it is also a profession. When we speak of a profession, we refer mainly to such things as the uses or applications of a body of knowledge. Sociologists play a rich and varied role in today's society. They serve in a variety of capacities, such as consultant, teacher, policy maker, researcher, administrator, clinical counsellor, social critic, interviewer, journalist, probation and parole worker, career counsellor, social worker, recreation worker, programme evaluator, urban planner, marketing administration coordinator, personnel manager, etc. They work in areas as broad and diverse as the discipline they have chosen.

A) Sociology and NGOs:

The literature on development nongovernmental organizations (NGOs) envisions an alternative form of social organization, one that is more altruistic, more cooperative, and less hierarchical than governments and for-profit organizations. We engage with the literature on quite different terms: NGOs and their donors are organizations, and much of what is distinctive about them as organizations derives from the special uncertainties they face due to the environments in which they operate, the goals they pursue, and the social and material technologies they employ. We conclude that there are unexplored issues in the literature on development NGOs that sociologists, with their toolkit of theories and practices, are uniquely qualified to address.

1) Non-Government Organisations (NGOs) have emerged as important civil society actors at the grass roots. So far as the developmental activities are concerned. The non-governmental organisations or the private voluntary organisations are basically non-profit making bodies whose primary aim is to contribute to the reduction of human sufferings and the development of the poor and the marginalised groups. They are an integral part of both the national and global civil society as they include local communities, cooperatives, church groups, trade unions, environment groups and consumer associations, women's groups, peasant leagues, as well as international organisations like Amnesty International, Oxfam, Friends of the Earth, etc.

2) These organisations are best known for their relief, educational, lobbying, human rights, health, employment generation, and poverty reduction activities. They are growing at a very fast rate in the developing parts of the world due to the increasing disillusionment especially of the poor with the government. The market has also failed to serve the interests of these vulnerable sections of the population. As a result many hopes have been placed on the NGOs, also known as the "third sector". NGOs are conceptualised as non-profit and nongovernmental organisations. Anheier and Salaman highlight some of the common characteristics of NGOs. According to them NGOs are:

a) Organisations, i.e., they have an institutional presence and structure; the state;

b) Non-profit distributing, i.e., they do not return profits to their managers or to a set of owners;

c) Self-governing, i.e., they are fundamentally in – control of their own affair; and

d) Voluntary, i.e., membership in them is not legally 'required and they attract some level of voluntary contribution of time or money.

It is significant that the element of private is to be understood in a very limited sense. It means that NGOs are neither part of the government apparatus and public administration nor are they dominated by public officials. Nor are they a private enterprise to earn profit. Indeed they have the social objective of providing selfless service to the millions, especially in those areas of activity where the state has either not been able to reach out, or has not been effective in providing service as per the local requirement and has withdrawn. At times the state has looked for collaborative arrangement with the NGOs to provide much needed service to the people, especially to the marginalised section of society.

3) Paul Streeten after examining the functioning of the NGOs in the developing societies claims that NGOs have certain advantages in promoting development at the grassroots. This is mostly because of the fact that:

a) NGOs are good for reaching and mobilising the poor and remote communities.
b) NGOs are participatory in their approach and follow a 'bottom up' strategy for the implementation of projects at the grassroots.
c) They are more innovative, flexible and experimental than the government's agencies.
d) The NGOs' projects are cost effective and efficient.
e) The NGOs promote sustainable development.
f) They are potentially organising and representative bodies in civil societies.

However, there has been a wide gap between the ideal image of NGOs and their modes of functioning at the grassroots. Indeed, the ideal-typical image of the NGOs has been widely demystified by several researchers. It has been pointed out that even though the NGOs work in the name of the poor, in effective terms they reinforce the rule of the power elite, incur a higher administrative cost, impose an autocratic, top down and non-participatory approach to development. Again, NGOs are not financially independent.

As most of the NGOs flourished under a charismatic leadership or are a body of dedicated workers, many of the project, collapse with the disappearance of such leaders and workers. It has also been pointed out that NGOs have no clear-cut objectives that they suffer from the problems of sustainability, and non- replicability; and being small they reach only a few people in developing countries. They fail to reach 80% of the 1.3 billion estimated to be living in extreme poverty. Even the much publicised Grameen Bank of Bangladesh, often cited as a model NGO, accounts for only 0.15% of national credit and all NGOs in Bangladesh together provide only 0.6% of total Credit.

It is important to mention that NGOs are to work in a context and to interact with various forces. They are largely dependent on the government and the international agencies for funds. They are also to interact with the local level politicians. At times their plans and programmes are framed, modified and executed under the influence of these politicians. NGOs' activities are also conditioned by localised culture and values of the marginalised people among whom they are working.

B) Sociology and Social Work:

Sociology & Social Work are the two disciplines concerned with social problems, social structure and how individuals respond to and live within cultural and structural limitations. If we look closer to both the terms, both of them deal with the relationship between Theory & Practice. Theory and practice are often mutually exclusive. If one deals with theory, it might be interpreted as one cannot at the same time work practically. On the other hand, when we act in practical work, the theoretical background is often overlooked. Hence; how do Theory & Practice interplay within the disciplines of Social Work and sociology?

Social work is a profession concerned with the aim to solve personal, family, community problems to attain satisfying personal, group and common relationships through social work practice. Sociology is the scientific study of society. It focuses on human interaction & inter-relationship between different groups, resources & development in the society. Social work deals with the individual and social problems in reference to the theoretical knowledge of sociology. Both sociology and social work look at the society as a network of social relationship. Sociology provides scientific analyze of society and social problems whereas, Social work provides most scientific and suitable means and methods to help people with problems. Sociology means understanding & classifying problems while; by analyzing those problems, Social work solves it. Sociology studies relationship and problems between people and society to maintain and establish social adjustments. If sociology studies relation and problems between individuals or society, social work helps those individuals and society to maintain and establish adjustment with the help of social work methods like case work, group work and community organization. Let's shed the light on the relationship between social work and sociology with relevant example: Generation Gap. Sociology analyses the relationship between teenagers with their parents, the role of modernization among teenagers, socialization and parenting process, problems faced by teenagers and parents due to communication gaped. On the other hand, social worker deals with parents or teenagers as clients, who has adjustment problem in the family. Social worker, along with the client, designs plan in the reference to social work method. Hence; Sociology viewed as a theoretical discipline and social work as practical profession, in the above ways, they interrelate with each other.

C) Sociology and Social Welfare:

Social Welfare can be defined both as a system and as an overall effort. This means that it can be designed as a systematic set of programs that assist the population in different stages of their lives but, that system comes from an effort and intention to provide that social welfare situation on the first place. Overall, social welfare means an ongoing attempt to take care of particular needs identified in the society. There are many different social welfare programs and they are implemented very differently depending on the country that we are looking at. There are unemployment care programs, elderly-people programs, retirement programs; assistance for disabled individuals, widow's care, among a wide range of support efforts most frequently developed as part of a government agenda to attend those particular situations.

This welfare assistance programs are designed by first researching the population and then addressing the problems identified by the study of its dynamics. Within each state, social welfare systems may go by different names, but they often serve similar functions. This can cause confusion when attempting to compare one state's program to another. Additionally, the requirements to qualify also vary, depending on the poverty line in a particular state. This allows for adjustments based on items such as cost of living that are not standardized across the country.

D) Sociology and Labour Welfare:

Labour Welfare concept is basically based on human values where each citizen has a right to work in a congenial environment with no hazards to his health on reasonable wages and other terms and conditions of employment. The days are over when labour was considered to be a commodity. The policy was of hire and fire and it was purely a master servant relationship. The country's independence, our constitutional structure, the advice of the International Labour Organization, the efforts of the Planning Commission- all these factors have greatly contributed to labour welfare. The Directive Principals and the Five Year Plans have created a new image for labour and its welfare. Various legislation which have come up have greatly helped in raising their standard of living and have given them a place of respect welfare founds specially have been created in several industries for the benefit of labour. The labour welfare officers have the responsibility to look after proper enforcement of such measures.

E) Sociology and Corporate Sector:

One of the most significant yet scarcely explored careers, sociology owns enormous potential with bright career opportunities for students who are interested in exploring culture, society and politics and their influence on people in depth. Sociology scope in India is especially enormous as it is a country full of diverse cultures and socio-political segments, which candidates might want to explore while working in sociology jobs. Contrary to popular perception, sociology is not a restrictive career. Rather opens the door to countless career opportunities in diverse fields. From media to activism, sociology scope in India is as expansive as a spectrum, holding diverse opportunities for candidates to learn their potential in a suitable field and follow the same. In order to have a career in sociology or BA sociology jobs after completing your degree, learn more about the field.

Sociology is the study of changes in social life, social causes, and effects of human behaviour on society. It also teaches students the method to investigate different structures, such as groups of people, institutions, and society as an entity.

Sociology also helps students develop critical thinking skills and the ability to measure and gather both quantitative and qualitative evidence. Besides, sociology as a platform for a career is growing at pace in India.

F) Sociology and Civil Services:

Indian Civil Services like IAS, IPS and IFS are also good options for these graduates as their main subject is sociology. For that, they should qualify the Civil Service Aptitude Test (CSAT) held by Union Public Service Commission. They can also write the exams conducted by State Public Service Commission and get into various administrative posts like

1) Assistant Commissioner
2) Block Development Officer
3) Tehsil Welfare Officer
4) Sub-divisional Magistrate
5) District Public Relation Officer

G) Sociology and Law:

Sociologists study human social relationships and institutions, using sophisticated computer programs to assemble and analyze their data. The research skills that a person acquires in a sociology bachelor's degree program provide a useful foundation for many different legal careers, but additional education and training in a specific legal specialty are required for entry into most legal careers.

1) Sociology and Law Connection:

A field called sociology of law, also known as socio-legal studies, became a recognized subspecialty within sociology in the 1930s. Two divisions of the American Sociological Association, the Section on Crime, Law and Deviance and the Section on Sociology of Law, reflect sociologists' continuing research on legal careers and other legal topics. Undergraduate sociology majors interested in entering a legal profession may wish to join these sections as student members. They may also choose sociology major with a specific focus on legal issues to learn more about the relationship between sociology and law.

2) Many Legal Careers Available:

People who have completed a sociology bachelor's degree should review legal careers they find attractive and then enroll in an appropriate legal education program. A license to practice will be necessary after completing law school if you're interested in becoming an attorney. Sociologists are well-suited to legal careers because they understand how laws and social institutions influence individual and group behavior. Transferrable skills include critical thinking, analytical reasoning and problem solving. Law and sociology jobs are usually conducted in one of three work settings: law firms, the criminal justice system, and federal, state and local government agencies.

a) Lawyer
b) Army JAG Corps
c) Judge
d) Paralegal

e) Law librarian
f) Private investigator
g) Legal secretary
h) Police officer
i) Detective
j) Parole officer

3) **Contact Legal Organizations:**
Because legal careers vary widely in terms of job titles and tasks, consulting members of the local branches of legal professional associations is the fastest way to find out whether a particular legal career might be a good fit. For example, paralegals frequently hold monthly dinner meetings in many cities under the sponsorship of organizations like the National Federation of Paralegal Associations and are usually willing to answer questions at these gatherings from people interested in entering the paralegal profession.

4) **Time and Money Investment:**
Among the factors that sociology majors need to consider in entering a legal profession is the amount of time and money they wish to invest in their legal education. People who want to become paralegals are usually required to enter one of four different types of academic programs: a paralegal certificate program that may last 6 weeks to 18 months, a 2-year associate degree program, a 4-year bachelor's degree program or a 2-year master's degree curriculum. Future lawyers must enter a full-time, 3-year doctoral degree program or spend 4 years attending part-time evening classes.

H) Sociology and Correctional Administration:

The study of crime and the careers of criminal offenders has been for many years a subject of sociological research. Investigations extend back to a period when sociologists brought to the study of social problems the enthusiasm and zeal of social reformers, and have contributed extensive research knowledge of criminal behavior. However, students of criminology are repeatedly faced with an interesting paradox. As a result of the sociologist's preoccupation with problems of social organization, it is reasonable to expect that sociological research in a special problem area, such as criminology, would first focus attention on the organizational aspects of the field. In criminology the major organizational problems are to be found in the structure and operation of correctional agencies. Yet these problems have received relatively little study by sociologists.

Sociologists have investigated extensively the differential incidence of crime in the community. They have made comparative studies of the crime rates in different societies and in urban and rural areas. The ecological distribution of crime within urban areas has been thoroughly explored. Sociologists have made de¬ tailed studies of special crime problems such as prostitution, sex delinquency, alcoholism, narcotic addiction, professional criminality, gang behavior, and racketeering. Many studies have been made of the correlates of crime such as broken homes, nationality and race, intelligence, physiological, economic, and psychological factors. These factors have been related to the incidence of crime in the community and the development of criminal careers. Detailed case studies have been undertaken and authentic personal documents obtained to reveal significant factors in the criminal environment. Special studies of the development and operation of criminal behavior systems have been made. More recently, sociologists have carried out extensive studies of white collar crime, that is, criminal violations in the world of business. In short, sociologists have devoted almost their entire research effort to the study of crime in the community, with a view to explaining the causes of crime, or the cultural and social factors which account for the development of criminal careers.

This situation is paradoxical to students of criminology, because the channelizing of research effort has prevented an exploration of the field of corrections which the sociologist is uniquely equipped to investigate. Failure to devote an equal amount of research attention to correctional problems has retarded the development of systematic knowledge of criminal behavior. In all the personal documents which sociologists have gathered from criminal offenders, the experience of arrest, trial, and incarceration has played a particularly significant part in the development of the criminal career. This insight has been securely established through analysis of the documentary material, but sociologists have failed to carry out adequate research investigations which would afford detailed knowledge of the character of this experience.

I) Sociology and Journalism:

In opinion, good journalism and good sociology have a lot in common, but there are important distinctions. Some excellent sociological work is actually done by journalists. The following points are not exhaustive, nor are they intended to be a set of rules, but they do provide a general guide to the distinctions between sociology and journalism.

1) In Journalism, Time is of the Essence:

One of the purposes of journalism is to let us know what happened that day, or increasingly what is happening right now. Sociology has the luxury of time: if you ever noticed, research published in journals was typically conducted at least a year earlier. And if a study is based on a large data set, say from the census or another government agency, it is likely to be at least two to three years old. This does not mean that research is necessarily outdated; sociology is about analysis and reflection, for which we need time. Journalism often includes analysis, but rarely are stories reflected on years later unless they are major events, like the attacks of September 11th or the aftermath of hurricane Katrina.

2) In Sociology, Data Collection is Systematic and Grounded in Theory:

Have you ever seen a news segment where they ask passersby on the street about an event of the day to try and grasp public opinion? While this might give the appearance of a random sample, it certainly is not. What street are the reporters standing on, and when? What kinds of people might be available for interviewing, and who might not ever go into that area? Who is willing to appear on camera, and who is not? When we have taught research methods we talk about this and there are always a few people who insist that this is as good a way as any to find out what "average" people are thinking. While such on-the-street interviews might add some color to a story, sociologists tend to employ more rigorous sampling methods. In one study we worked on years ago, we purchased the customer list from a utility company and selected every fourth household to participate in the study. Is this a perfect, fool-proof method? Of course not. Some people might have had their gas or electricity cut off, and as we found out, the list provided addresses that did not exist. Conducting ethnographic research is a lot like in-depth reporting, although sociologists tend to spend much longer with a group that journalists might (although this is not always the case). Journalists spending time with a group in their everyday environment might also incorporate information about the broader context, but sometimes the purpose is just to better understand what it is like to be in their shoes. This is true of sociological research too, but more often than not sociologists attempt to connect their findings to a theory, or sometimes they create one of their own based on their findings. Yes, journalists might bring in theories too, but this is less common than in sociology.

3) Journalists' Work is aimed at a Wide Audience:

Just as often think journalists can include more contextual information in reporting, sociologists can learn a lot from how journalists present their findings. Journalists do focus on different audiences and thus go into varying levels of depth; for instance, on television the local news has a different target than Charlie Rose, and in print the Wall Street Journal's coverage varies from USA Today's. If you have read the two newspapers you can spot the difference right away. Even if journalists focus on a niche audience, it is almost always larger than the audience sociologists tend to write for. Monte Bute wrote a very provocative review in Contexts, a sociology magazine that aims to reach a larger audience than just sociologists. He describes a study that found in recent decades, articles published in major sociology journals have become more jargon-filled and less accessible to general audiences. The attempt to solidify sociology's stature in social science has had one major downside: it makes for dry reading and therefore has a limited audience. We know for some people, and perhaps for some research, this is just fine. But sociological thinking should not be out of reach, and should instead become more available to the public. One way to do this is to promote writing that is engaging and informative without being overly superficial. It takes years to unlearn the tendency to write in the passive voice, to remove all traces of the author's voice and use enough jargon to prove that you know the lingo. Ethnographers tend to also write well, as if losing the pretense of total objectivity gives one license to tell a good story. Journalists and sociologists have a lot to learn from one and other. Hopefully in the future journalists will make greater use of sociological research and thinking in their reporting and will also provide their readers with a greater understanding of the general context that informs their stories. For this to happen, sociologists have to broaden our scope and target our findings more generally, and yes, we also need to become better at communicating our ideas. Both journalists and sociologists study who, what, where, when and why; it's the "how" where we tend to differ.

J) Sociology and Human Resource Management:

A sociology degree provides you with skills that transfer to the profession of human relations. How applicable your degree is for HR depends on the area of HR you want to enter.

For example, your sociology degree will be more relevant if you want to go into diversity or sensitivity training, workforce development or succession planning. Reviewing aspects of sociology that can be helpful to you in your professional life in HR helps you better prepare for these types of jobs.

1) Basic Areas of Human Resources:

HR professionals can work as generalists, handling most or all of the department's payroll, recruiting, training and other administrative functions, and this often happens at smaller companies with lower budgets. A generalist who doesn't have a needed expertise outsources the function but still oversees the department. HR specialists, on the other hand, work in specific areas, explains jobs website Indeed.com. These include functions such as:

a) Recruiting
b) Training
c) Payroll administration
d) Benefits and compensation
e) Wellness
f) Legal compliance
g) Sensitivity and diversity training

2) How Sociology Applies to HR:

Sociology is basically the study of humans, particularly as they behave in communities and societies. A workplace has its own culture, micro-communities (management and staff) and a host of interpersonal relationship issues that companies need to address. Therefore, a degree in sociology can be valuable to companies looking to build and maintain an effective workforce, explains the University of California Berkeley Sociology Department. HR skills include interviewing employees, conducting surveys, analyzing the results, recommending policies, providing employee training, and creating company policy guides and employee handbooks.

The larger the company, the more valuable a sociology degree holder will be for a human resources department. This is because larger companies spend more money and training on building complex workforces and managing them.

****

Review Questions

Q.1 Answers in 100 Words:

1) Explain the Concept of Applied Sociology.
2) State the Career Opportunities in Social Work for Sociology.
3) Write Note on Sociology and Social Welfare.
4) State the Career Opportunities in Corporate Sector for Sociology.
5) Explain the Relation between Sociology and Correctional Administration.

Q.2 Answers in 200 Words:

1) Discuss about the Career Opportunities in NGOs for Sociology.
2) State the Career Opportunities in Law for Sociology.
3) Explain the Career Opportunities in Journalism for Sociology.
4) Discuss about the Sociology and Human Resource Management.

Q.3 Answers in 300 Words:

1) What is Applied Sociology? Explain the Scope of Applied Sociology.
2) Explain the various Career Opportunities with Sociology.

Q.4 Write Short Note on Following:

1) Applied Sociology.
2) Sociology and Civil Services.
3) Sociology and Lobour Welfare.
4) Sociology and Law Connection.

****

NOTES